Unforgettable

Unforgettable

A Son, a Mother, and the Lessons of a Lifetime

SCOTT SIMON

FLATIRON
BOOKS
NEW YORK

www.flatironbooks.com

The Library of Congress Cataloging-in-Publication Data is available upon
request.

ISBN 978-1-250-06113-3 (hardcover)
ISBN 978-1-250-06115-7 (e-book)

Flatiron books may be purchased for educational, business, or promotional
use. For information on bulk purchases, please contact the Macmillan
Corporate and Premium Sales Department at 1-800-221-7945, extension
5442, or write to specialmarkets@macmillan.com.

First Edition: March 2015

10 9 8 7 6 5 4 3 2 1

To all those kind, tough, and loving souls in hospitals who do so much for those we love and see us through to the end

Author's Note

Mother called: "I can't talk. I'm surrounded by handsome men." Emergency surgery. If you can hold a thought for her now . . .

I have covered a lot of wars, and try to be careful about comparing combat to anything else. But wars and final illnesses both have moments of panic spaced between hours of tedium. There can be a lot of waiting and staring off into space.

It was in these times, during what turned out to be the last days of my mother's life, that I began to post messages on Twitter. I think I wrote these 140-character lines for distraction, for companionship, and because although my world had pretty much shrunk to the confines of a single room in an intensive care unit, what I heard, saw, and felt there touched on the universal experience of life and death (an overworked phrase that's apt for once).

My mother was also just so funny and *interesting*. I wanted to share what she said, to make people laugh and think, especially as I began to feel that my mother was giving a last great performance—it certainly was one for our small family. She was also an old showgirl who had been married to a comedian and had a son who is a broadcaster. My mother was *not* a shrinking violet. She knew she was giving us great material. I don't believe anything I wrote, then or now, violates her privacy. I hope it reveals, for others to enjoy, my mother's humor, spirit, wisdom, and the pleasure of her company.

I have left the Tweets unchanged, including whatever typos I thumbed at the time. I have sometimes rearranged where they appear in the timeline of events, as I often did not post a Tweet for hours after whatever prompted it.

I am one of those people who really do walk around with a notebook. But when I flew to join her in the hospital, I did not know my mother would die there; in fact, I hoped my arrival might help spring her from the ICU. I did not know I would write this book. I did not take reportorial notes, and often a few scrawled words would represent a conversation of many minutes. I rely on the intensity of those days, a practiced memory, and a son's love to reconstruct here what my mother said with accuracy and clarity.

I have kept a lot of names, but resorted to just first names in many cases, and changed a few where it seems wise or kind. I have changed the names of all doctors.

All mistakes are mine and mine alone. My mother worked hard to rear a son who can say that.

1

Our children want to know if you're dead forever. I tell them yes. But I wonder about that too.

Death makes life worthwhile. It gives each moment meaning. I hope I live to one hundred and fifty, and that our daughters can make it to at least two hundred. But death drives life. It frightens and inspires us. Do away with death, and we'd have no reason to get out of bed (or into it), grow, work, or love. Why would we do much of anything if we had the time for everything? It's the certainty of death that moves us to sing and write poems, find friends, and sail across oceans and skies. It's because we know that we don't have all the time in the world that we try to use the uncertain and unknowable time that we have to do something that endures. Death is sad, grim, unwelcome, and invaluable. But it's why we try to make something of life. It's why we have children.

I don't know what becomes of us when we die. But I believe I will go on to a place (which will probably look a lot like Chicago and Normandy) where I'll find my mother and my father, my stepfather, and all of our beloved cats, dogs, horses, turtles, and fish who predecease me. I'll get to take a walk with Gandhi, have a glass of D'Yquem with Mr. Jefferson, and a glass of just about anything with Sir Winston. I'll get together over tea and an asp with Cleopatra. I'll have a catch with Jackie Robinson (and hope that celestial climes improve my infield skills).

I believe that I'll get to look out over the world and behold my daughters. They'll feel my love, hearten to hear my gentle instruction, and miss me; but not so much that they won't spend most of their time giggling and enjoying life in full measure.

In time, I believe I'll be reunited with my fabulously kind and beautiful wife, even if she runs away with a Hollywood star or an Italian race car driver as soon as my ashes cool. I will count on heavenly powers of understanding to look down at her happiness and nobly smile, and if he expects to be with her too, I rely on God to work that out.

I do not know if God will reveal Him, Her, or Itself to me as a craggy old African man with a long white beard, or a mature, Rubenesque woman barely concealed by clouds, or as some kind of mollusk. I am undecided on the essential questions that can make theologians stammer: If there is a God, how does He or She or It let little children suffer? What kind of Heaven can there be if innocents have to share it with scoundrels? Do gnats have souls?

But when I spent the last days of my mother's life alongside her in the intensive care unit, our talk about death and whatever follows grew real. The hereafter was no longer hypothetical. It was the stop just ahead, and the next place I knew my mother would be (and the rest of us, too, in too short a time).

My vision of the hereafter has no scientific, religious, or even much mythical foundation. But I just can't get by, day after day, thinking that we go on to nothing when we're done here, and that we'll never again see those we love. I don't worry about being right. I just want to wrap myself in a belief that gets me through the long nights of life.

I am getting a life's lesson about grace from my mother in the ICU. We never stop learning from our mothers, do we?

2

**Huge black fly in my wife's wine. She picks up fly &
and says, "Spit it out!" Old Irish joke in my family
works in French.**

We turned the key, and got a call. We'd rented a house in California wine country for summer vacation and invited my mother to join us. She was eighty-four and had been declared cancer-free after a rough round of radiation treatments. We imagined how she'd ooh and aah through farmers' markets, watch our daughters ride horses and muck stables, and sip her Rob Roy (scotch and sweet vermouth, with a maraschino cherry lowered like a depth charge into the center) looking over serene green vineyards.

She'd had good luck in recent years, and plenty of reverses. She had a happy third marriage (adding to what she called her "railroad train of a name," Patricia Lyons Simon Newman Gelbin). She'd had cancer surgery; it worked. She loved her daughter-in-law and treasured her two grandchildren.

But my mother had also lost half a lung to cancer. She'd seen so many friends depart she said she didn't want to answer the phone. "They say, 'Hi, Pat, I'm Betsy's niece, and I'm sorry to tell you . . .'" She had a constant cough no doctor could fathom, felt tired and winded, and often fell down. She'd slipped on ice coming back from a physical therapy session, lost six teeth, and got a great big purple eggplant of a bruised eye (I called her Rocky). She had dental surgery and eye stitching, and when all that had healed, she fell out of a kitchen chair while reading the newspaper (we told her: listen to the radio). She got depressed at the idea she would never feel well again.

And then little nits of cancer—on the x-ray, they looked like dim, distant stars—began to glimmer in her one good lung.

"Guess I'll do whatever I have to do," she said, which were radiation sessions where she was trussed up like a Christmas goose and zapped for half an hour with a ray strong enough to peel paint—or kill cancer.

"You always come roaring back," we told her. "Like a lioness."

"I'm more likely to have a small little bark, like a poodle," she said.

"You'll live to be a hundred. People do nowadays."

"Not like this."

So we'd reached that point where my wife and I began to say, "Let's see Grand-mère"—what our daughters called her; Caroline, my wife, is French—"as much as possible." But all of my mother's trials only made us think of her as strong. She had survived bruises, spills, cancer, grief, and sorrows, and just kept going.

She was getting ready to join us in California when she noticed she had lost about twenty pounds—without trying—and so she brought her blue jeans to a seamstress and her body to the hospital for a blood test. She'd read an article that said tuberculosis was on the rise; weight loss and a constant cough were among the symptoms. She didn't want to put our daughters at risk.

The blood test didn't reveal tuberculosis. But the doctors didn't like what they saw. We had turned the key to the house when Matthew, my mother's husband, called.

"Your mom is in the hospital."

"What's wrong?"

"Nothing. They just didn't like what they saw."

"What did they see?"

"They don't know. But she can't fly out tomorrow. . . ."

By the time I spoke to my mother a few hours later, she seemed more distressed that the airline would exact a fee to change her flight than about her condition.

(I see now that this may have been an act.)

"They get you every damn which way these days, don't they?" she asked me.

Still, she was eighty-four.

"Still, maybe I should . . ."

"No." Her voice was firm. "Your daughters deserve a vacation with their father. Besides, I'll be out in just a few days."

A few more days passed. I kept my mother informed about all the daughters, dogs, and horses, and how there were radishes as big as baseballs and strawberries as red as lipstick in the fields just outside our windows.

One morning my mother called before dawn. We could still hear coyotes whine (they make you flinch, like mewling children) in the hills above the vineyards.

"Darling, I can't talk now," she said. "I'm surrounded by handsome men. They're taking me in for surgery—well, you know, they don't like to call it surgery, that gets people worried, so they call it a *surgical procedure*—but they're putting me to sleep to put a camera into my lung and take a look at something."

"Smile" is all I could think to tell her.

My mother called again a few hours later to say doctors had detected a mysterious dark something in her one good lung. It could be a fungus, it could be scarring—or it could be cancer.

"I think I better . . ."

"*Don't,*" my mother said in a scolding tone she knew made a difference with me. "Matthew is with me. I'll be fine. Look, darling, this isn't the end," she said. "This thing in my lung—that may be the end of me. But even if it's cancer again, we'll have some time."

But during all this time, we heard just about nothing from any doctor. We were told that a pulmonologist who had once diagnosed her with cancer was overseeing her care. She stopped in to see my mother once, and never returned my (increasingly truculent) phone messages. I'd get an occasional call back from one or another young resident who had at least seen my mother. But whole days went by when my mother said no doctor had looked in on her. The nurses were attentive and considerate, but she felt that doctors just didn't want to bother.

I left a message for the pulmonologist: "When our cat was spayed, the vet called twice a day. Is one call a week too much to ask for a patient who's under intensive care?"

(That message didn't work either.)

So I told my mother I was going to get on a plane. This time she didn't argue.

"I just want to get this cleared up, whatever it is, good or bad, and go home." Then she added, "There's a show at the Museum of Contemporary Art"—it was across the street from the hospital—"that we could see, anyway."

My wife was driving me to the San Francisco airport when one of the young residents phoned.

"Your mother doesn't want any more care," she announced.

"But I just spoke to her. She sounded strong. She's tired of all the uncertainty and wants to go home, of course," I began, and the resident jumped in.

"She said she doesn't want anything else done for her."

"That's not possible. I know she doesn't want any extreme measures, but aren't we a ways from that?"

My wife bore down on twisting roads. Our hearts thumped in our ears.

"She says she doesn't want anything more."

"I have her power of attorney," I told her. "I'm empowered to make medical decisions for her." But the resident persisted.

"I talked to a senior physician. He says we have to follow what your mother said. She wants no more care."

I erupted.

"I think you heard my mother say she's tired and wants to go home. You just heard certain code words and think she's saying she wants no more care. Can't you hear that she's fighting to find out what's wrong?"

I was mad, loud, and no doubt insufferable.

"If you're going to be a good doctor someday," I shouted, "you have to listen with your heart! She wants help. Help her!"

I phoned my mother and struggled to sound unruffled.

"What time do you land?" she asked.

"About ten."

"If you go straight to Rick's," she said of a friend's restaurant, "I'll bet you can still get a margarita."

She didn't sound like a woman who wanted out. But I boarded

the plane in San Francisco wondering—based on the word of a young resident with tin ears—if those would be my mother's last words to me.

New family motto: no tamale left behind.

3

My mother knows the name & story of every nurse & doctor in the ICU. She keeps no one a stranger.

I heard it so often when I was growing up: "Your mom's no milk-and-cookies mother," although she happened to bake terrific cookies (including Chicago Gingerbread Bears for the Super Bowl, with orange icing numerals for 34 [Payton], 9 [McMahon], and a supersized 72 [William "The Refrigerator" Perry]).

My mother was glamorous. She'd worked in nightclubs; she'd modeled; she'd dated mobsters; she was a divorced, single mother (when that was considered slightly racy) who had been married to a comedian. She also was a secretary, a typist, and an ad agency receptionist in the *Mad Men* era.

She sold clothes in posh shops on Michigan Avenue. Carl Sandburg patted her fanny and she had a date with Gene Kelly (if either had led anywhere I might have been a better poet or dancer).

My mother was at the famous, furtive Rat Pack concert at the Villa Venice that Frank, Dean, and Sammy did for their godfather, Sam Giancana. It was an offer that they—and my mother—couldn't refuse.

She was the Jon James Hairspray Girl and the Archway Cookies Mother. She was the pert Midwestern mom who sat, mute and smiling, next to a fair-haired husband and a freckled son (not me) in a baseball cap while brawny-voiced men sang, pirate-style, "Go with Sohio!" (a local gas). She was the gal in a spangled dress at the Chicago Auto Show who ran a hand over a fender and said, "The new Chevrolet. Sleek, powerful, and economical."

Spending twelve hours on high heels in a loud, dark, smoky club, hauling soggy Chicago winter coats in and out of a closet and sidestepping the fanny-pats of patrons who assume a cover charge includes "covering" the hostess, is not as arduous as mining coal for a living. But it's also not glamorous.

My mother was a working girl. We lived in a one-bedroom apartment with radiators that clanged and coughed and a shower that ran hot and cold when the toilet flushed. She rode the bus. She packed her lunch—and often went without lunch toward the end of the month to pay the rent on the first.

(But she made sure that I had breakfast, lunch, dinner, and a staggering assortment of after-school snacks.)

The Jon James (a local drugstore brand, not to be confused with L'Oréal) Hairspray Girl spent most of that ten-hour photo shoot shivering in lingerie under a rain slicker while a crew sprayed water into a fan and blew it into her delicate face, to show how the miraculous Jon James kept the beautiful brunette's hairdo beauty-shop fresh in a raging rainstorm (in fact, her hair was held in place with clear industrial varnish; when my mother washed her hair that night it came out in chunks, along with hunks of her hair).

My mother had cool hands that could have been from a sculpture in the Musée Rodin. Instead, she was the thumb under the Royal Crown and Diet Rite Cola Save-A-Seal (before that meant saving real, honking Arctic seals). Hers were the hands that wrung a dozen *perfectly formed cubes* out of the *amazing flexible ice tray,* and plunked beautifully balanced scoops of Stewart's Private Blend Coffee into a pot. Her hands zipped zippers, folded fresh, sweet-smelling laundry, and held a scrubber, sword-like, above a toilet bowl.

The term for this kind of modeling is "hand jobs." Imagine being the kid in the seventh grade whose mother does hand jobs.

My mother sold rags, too, up and down Michigan Avenue: boutique, couture, women's sportswear, men's suits, prom dresses, wedding dresses, and debutantes' gowns. Many of her fashion commandments still ring in my mind when I step into my closet:

- Quality lasts.
- Dressing poorly calls attention to your clothes. Dressing well does not.
- Better to be slightly overdressed than underdressed. Who knows what the day will bring? If you wind up meeting the Duchess of Cambridge, Frieda Pinto, or the cardinal of Chicago—or get taken to a hospital emergency room—do you want to be a well-dressed man in a blazer, or some guy wearing an Arctic Monkeys SUCK IT AND SEE T-shirt?
- Dress for the job you want, not the one you have.
- If you wear solid colors for a photograph, you won't cringe when you see yourself years later.
- There's usually a reason something is on sale.

My mother sold fur coats to men and their giggling gal pals on Friday nights, and took them in return Monday morning. She sold opulent party frocks that needed elaborate tailoring to women who said, "But only if you get it to me in Wilmette by Thursday night." So my mother schlepped them herself, often taking me along on the train (there was a famous pancake shop near the station). One of the reasons my mother always left a good tip (and why I hope I do) is the memory of people (and to be fair, there were just a few) who would open the door for their dress and say, "It's about time," and close it on my mother's smile.

She was a secretary at an ad agency when an account executive told her, "Patti, honey baby, help us out with something here." For the next couple of hours, my mother's hands pointed to a frozen chicken Kiev, varnished to glisten, for one shot, and in the next to the hot, delicious version, oozing steam and butter (the steam was puffed in with a vaporizer; the butter was unchilled lemon Jell-O, speckled with chopped chives).

She came home with a box of twenty frozen chicken Kievs. We fit half a dozen in our small freezer after scraping frost from the sides with a soup spoon, and squeezed another ten into our small oven and rang the doorbells of our fifth-floor neighbors. Chicken Kiev Night at the Simons'! Neighbors traipsed in bearing bottles of scotch, wine, and Sara Lee cheesecakes pulled from their freezers.

In the lunchroom at school the next day, most of my pals pulled out peanut butter and jelly sandwiches. I unwrapped three chicken Kievs.

"Try 'em," I told them. "Bite it and it squirts butter."

"Oooh," said my friend Billy Leavitt. "Bite me and I'll squirt butter, too."

My mother and I would laugh whenever we remembered all this.

"Some nights we barely had a can of soup, right, baby?" she would say. "And some nights it was chicken Kiev."

I just realized: she once had to let me go into the big wide world. Now I have to let her go the same way.

4

**All hospitals should have roll-out chairs in ICU
rooms so loved ones can spend night w/ patients &
not sleep on floor. @NMHnews**

We landed about an hour late. My phone rang as I sped to the hospital in a taxi.

"Mamacita, why aren't you sleeping?"

"It's not that late," she protested like a teenager, and when I walked in a few minutes later, anxious and breathless, she was smiling and spirited.

"My little boy!" she told the nurse who lifted her by her shoulders and plumped the pillows behind her, and the nurse laughed.

"We've all been expecting you," she said. "All night we've been hearing, 'My son is on his way.'"

"Anne is the loveliest person," said my mother, and for the next fifteen minutes, my mother—who had a tube in her chest, tubes in her arms and up her nose—diverted all talk about herself. We heard more about Anne. My mother wanted to hear about her granddaughters. She asked what was in the news. When I told her that there was turmoil in Egypt and an earthquake in China, and that the Duke and Duchess of Cambridge had had their baby—a boy—my Irish mother raised her hands to her shoulders. The tubes in her arms clacked as they got tangled, and the lights on the monitors threaded into her arms began to bounce and blink.

"At last!" she said.

But when she brought her arms back to her bed, I could see the whorls of blue bruises where all the tubes bit the back of her hands and along her wrists. It looked like she had to gasp a breath out of what had become, for her, truly thin air before she could speak.

"How are you feeling?" I was finally able to ask.

My mother's hand trembled as she reached for a cup; I held her hand and brought it closer. She gurgled some water through a straw.

"I just wish someone would tell me what's going on."

"I can't find out either."

"The nurses are such lovely people. But they can't tell you much. Overnight especially, you know. They get overworked."

She paused for breath. She coughed. It looked like it took most of her strength to catch her breath and bottle up enough to speak again.

"If you need help—just if a pillow slips below your neck, and makes you sit forward—you have to call for help, which is a pain. But they have so many people to worry about. Who must be worse."

I thought of all the nights my mother had sat up with me.

"I'm going to spend the night," I announced. "I can plump pillows. I can get you water. If you need the nurses, I'll go get them."

"But you need a good night's sleep."

"So do you," I told her. "I'll be fine right here."

I sat back in a recliner that would be my bed for the night. It didn't recline.

"They had to change them all," Anne explained when she came in a little later and saw me squirm. "Someone fell out of one and sued."

"Lawyers," I said.

"Doctors," Anne laughed, and my mother said, "Doctors, lawyers, lawyers, doctors, let's call the whole thing off."

"Your mother is so funny," said Anne. "We've been having some great laughs together."

I stood up from the non-recliner. During my reportorial career, I'd slept in bunkers, mud hovels, ramshackle buses, and warlords' tents. The floor of an intensive care unit should be like a down mattress in a Swiss inn.

"Can I please have some pillows and blankets?"

Anne brought a bundle. I spread blankets on the floor and piled up two pillows for my head, and laid out two more for my trunk and bottom. It felt like . . . I was sleeping on the floor.

"Are you comfortable?" asked my mother, and I paused for best effect.

"I make a living."

"Har-dee-har-har." She gave a fake guffaw through her oxygen tubes.

I got up to fit the ends back into her nose and dabbed with a tissue.

"This is so embarrassing," my mother said.

"You used to dab a lot worse for me."

When she had leaned back again I told her, "I got the oddest call on my way here, from a resident. A Dr. Rhodes."

"Ah yes. Very pretty. Soft voice. I had to ask her to come closer and say things again."

"She said you didn't want any more care."

My mother leaned up for the cup of ice water, and I brought the straw to her lips.

"No. I said I was tired of just being left here. I want to know what's going on. I said if they weren't going to do anything, they might as well send me home."

"She heard something different."

"I'm not surprised," said my mother. "No one really listens to old people. We make people nervous."

At some point, we both grabbed odd minutes of sleep. There was a change of shift, and another nurse came in and wondered why a man was sleeping on the floor. I pulled myself into the non-recliner and tried to smile.

"You must be Scotty."

I must have nodded.

"Your mother is a peach," said a nurse named Hilda. "I'm glad she's getting some rest. But we've had some great conversations. She is the most interesting person, isn't she?"

I brought news to my Irish mother in hospital of the royal birth, & she said, "We have a king!" Always a UK, eh?

5

My mother & I just sang Que Sera Sera 3 times. God bless you Doris Day for giving us such a great theme song.

An intensive care unit in the middle of the night is not a good place to sleep. The whole floor is a racket of essential but frightful beeps, pings, and grim bleats from what sounds like some kind of ghastly pipe organ. Orange and green lights tease and blink. Nurses and technicians make necessary rounds to record vital signs and dispense medications. Doors slide back and forth, open and shut, and the wheels on heavy carts squeak up and down the hallways, like—I'm sorry, but this is the kind of thought that comes into your mind when you try to sleep on the floor at four in the morning—carts in old movies about the Black Plague.

"Why don't we try some music?" my mother proposed.

I was traveling with a small, sleek new tablet computer (which, by the time you read this, will seem humongous and ungainly).

"What would you like to hear?" I asked. "I should be able to download most anything."

"Oh, you know what I like."

"Judy. Tony Bennett," I suggested. "Ol' Blue Eyes. Nat."

"Nat," she said immediately. "Let's begin there."

"Stardust" came on first. My mother's eyes closed with the first swell of strings.

"High up in the sky the little stars climb . . ."

"That voice," she said softly. "His voice. So beautiful."

"Yes."

"I heard him a couple of times at the Chez Paree, you know. Like . . . every word was wrapped in silk . . ."

The tablet was on her nightstand and I was on the floor next to my mother's hospital bed, where the squeaky carts and purposeful nurses wouldn't roll over me while Nat King Cole wrapped every song in satin. My pillow—and so my head—lay just in front of a toilet.

"I love you for sentimental reasons . . ."

I heard my mother's breathing snag, and an ensemble of beeps. I flung off the blankets to stand and poke my hand around the rails of her bed to reach for hers.

"I'm fine, baby." She opened her eyes slightly. "Just listening. Isn't he beautiful? Go back to sleep."

I tightened my fingers.

"When I'm alone with only dreams of you that won't come true, what'll I do?"

We heard Nat King Cole's satin voice, and the sirens, clangs, and roars outside that are the stomach rumbles of a great city in the middle of the night. My mother pinched her fingers around her nose to waggle her oxygen tubes.

"It winds from Chicago to L.A. More than two thousand miles all the way. . . ."

"Nat was from here, you know."

"I remember."

"His daddy was a pastor on the South Side. I think his church was right near wherever Route Sixty-Six begins. Such a gentle-man. When his last set of the night was over, the service crew would bring out bottles of champagne and glasses for the band. 'Compliments of Mr. Cole.' And he'd sit with them a few minutes to say thanks. Offered his hand to everyone. A classy guy."

"That's what I always heard."

My mother turned her face toward the window, and its shut-tered blinds, but pressed on my fingers.

"I'm glad you're here." Her voice caught; got lower and softer. "I'm sorry to drag you away from the girls."

"I want to be here," I told her. "They want me to be here."

When my mother turned her head there were bubbles along the tip of her nose and her eyes were shiny. I drew out a hand to hold a tissue under her eyes, and the palm of my hand under her nose.

My mother asked, "Do you think we'll get out of this?"

I began to fumble words about doctors and tests before my mother just said, "I guess I will get out of this. One way or another . . ."

She didn't have to finish that punch line for the son of a co-median. My mother took my hand down to her bedcovers.

"Things are more fun with you here."

"It's fun to be with you. Look at the good time the nurses are having."

"We've always been able to make each other laugh," said my mother. "We've always been lucky that way, haven't we?"

She closed her eyes for a while and I crawled back down to the pillows on the floor, the flashing lights, the whimpering wheels, the whooshing doors, the grim pipe organ chorus, the fitful hiss of my mother's breaths, and the purr of Nat's songs.

"*Unforgettable, that's what you are. Unforgettable, though near or far . . .*"

I had crossed the thin line between waking up early and never quite going to sleep when the door was quietly pulled back and a woman entered just beyond a sliver of sunlight that had seeped through closed blinds.

"Oh, Blanca," said my mother.

"Good morning, Patricia," she softly replied.

Blanca tied off blue-and-white garbage sacks next to my mother's bedside, lifted them into a cart, and snapped out fresh sacks from a roll.

"I always look forward to seeing you, Blanca. Doesn't she have the most wonderful smile, Scotty?"

She did.

My mother introduced us. I got to my feet. I nodded to Blanca, who wore gloves to tie and haul hospital refuse, which discouraged the chivalrous instinct my mother had instilled in me to shake her hand. I said I was off to search for a cup of coffee and offered to bring back two more.

"No, thanks," said Blanca. "Your mother's so nice. She always cheers me up."

"You always cheer me up, Blanca," my mother told her.

Thanks for prayers for my mother in ICU. She greeted the woman who picks up trash: "Blanca, you herald a new day." Class.

6

In line at hospital Starbucks. Dancing in the Streets comes on. Line begins to sing, "They're dancin' in Chi-caw-go!"

Men and women wearing white coats and blue labels of the palliative care team arrived as I rounded the corner twenty minutes later.

I would get to know and like them. But waking up to see the palliative care team, like birds on a wire, doesn't usually signal a cheery day.

The team told my mother that they wanted to know what kind of care she wanted.

"I want them to find out what's going on," she said. "I walk in for a blood test, and I wind up like this. People stick pins into me, and put a tube in my chest, and never tell me what's going on."

"We see a Do Not Resuscitate order in your file."

"Oh that. Yes," my mother told them. "I've lived a good life. I don't want anything extreme. I don't want to bankrupt my family. But I'd like to find out what's going on. My son is here," she said, and tilted her head in my direction. "He'll make any decisions. I'm just tired of getting poked and prodded. No one tells me anything. I just want to get all of these tubes out of me and get out of here."

A palliative team member explained they could move her into another room in a wing that had a wonderful view of the city. It was on a high floor, above all the noise of bus farts, truck splats, and police whistles. She wouldn't be wired into the beeping, whirring, and clamorous contraptions they have in the ICU.

"But those machines are giving you a lot of support for your breathing," he said. "That's harder in this other wing. So let me ask," and he did so gently, "if you think you'd be more comfortable in this other place."

(He never used—never had to—a word like *hospice*.)

My mother scrunched up her face under the oxygen tubing in her nostrils.

"Maybe. I don't know. Let me think. Maybe if I knew what's going on."

"There are tests they can continue to do to try to find out what's going on."

"I'm sooo tired of tests!" my mother came back forcefully. "Why can't they just find out what's going on and get me out of here?"

"They might need a few more tests," said a doctor on the palliative team. "How do you feel about that?"

I had held myself back from topping off my mother's sentences. I figured the medical team needed to hear her words and see her spirit. But I felt it was now a son's job to step forward.

"My mother will go through any tests that might figure out what's going on," I told them. "She may grouse, because they're messy and painful. But whole days go by and she doesn't see a doctor. Then you guys walk in and ask if she wants to keep going.

If it's bad news, she can take it. But she'd like to keep trying until you can tell us *something.*"

A team doctor began to ask something else. My mother lifted her voice above his.

"I think this conversation is over," she told him, and I held myself back from cheering.

"You just saw a spirited woman," I told the doctors when we circled outside of my mother's room. "She's tired and wants to get out. So would you. But she's fighting! She's kvetching! She threw you out! When she says, 'I'm so tired of your tests, I don't want any more,' she means, 'I wish you'd figure out what the hell is wrong so you can fix it or so I can know what I have to face.' She wants to fight. That's why she's grousing. Listen with your hearts."

A week later, after my mother died, my wife and I found some scraps of paper she had at her bedside and saw these notes she had set down in her careful, looping, Catholic schoolgirl script. They were for an attorney we knew.

> *Not sure as to what I verbally agreed to yesterday from nurse and young . . . doctor as I am really sick.*

> *What to do and how to retract if necessary for both babbled technicals, went too quickly and I am really sick. But they immediately pasted a decal on me.*

> *Call if you can.*

I do not believe that other doctors or hospitals could have prolonged my mother's life for even another day, and certainly not to a standard she would have liked. But they might have spared her a lot of anxieties just by listening.

My mother was right: America pastes decals on old people. They are identified as a demographic group, a market, or a political lobby, but often feel invisible, unheard, and powerless as individuals. People talk past them, as we do to children. Their bodies start failing them, then fighting them. To be old in America is to live in a world in which you have to take pills but can't pry open the bottles, and can't open a drugstore pocket comb because it comes encased in protective packaging fit for the Agra Diamond. The elderly are accused of slurping up government benefits and medical care in a way that poisons our children's future. Every marketer and media company wants to suck up what's inside their wallets, but avoid the taint of being identified with the cranky, wrinkly oldsters. Intricate technologies bark at them from cold screens for passwords they can't (can any of us?) remember, and actions that might as well be commands in an ancient Parthian language.

My mother had come into a hospital for a quick stick in her finger to see if she was sick. She had planned to have lunch, and dawdle in front of the store windows; she had planned to fly to see her grandchildren the next day. But instead, she'd been whisked into a ward, jolted, jabbed, and speared without anyone she recognized as a doctor ever really saying why. And now my mother was being asked, in so many words, if she was ready to give up breathing to get a better view. Has medical care become so compartmentalized that the first inkling a patient gets that her case is untreatable is when the palliative care team circles the bed?

Anytime you've heard me being gracious & kind, it reflected my mother's teaching. Anytime I was unkind, I fell short.

7

My mother in ICU sees Kate & Will holding baby and tears: "Every baby boy is a little king to his parents." So I tear too.

The heart revises memories to fit the occasion, and there was no reason for my mother and me to use her deathbed to recall a lot of painful truths. During our colorful years of canned soup and chicken Kiev, my father was also drinking himself to death. My mother loved him, but she had to leave him before he could bring us all down in drink; then he died when I was sixteen. Her mother, who was also her best friend, had already taken her life, which had left my mother feeling abandoned with a young son, unsteady work, and a husband who was funny, sweet-natured, but destructive.

My mother met lots of other men during those years. Almost all of the ones I knew were kind and good. But the one she really loved was married; that left her feeling even lonelier. She eventually met and married two fine men, but only after, as she put it, "a lot of trial and error."

In my adult years, I've tried to imagine (for she kept all such worries from me) how many nights my mother must have spent staring at the ceiling from the springs in her sofa bed, figuring how to make it to the end of the month. The days she went without breakfast or lunch (which I never did) so I could have a dinner of cauliflower with shrimp cocktail sauce (a course my mother devised when she observed that the real appeal of a shrimp cocktail for me was the sauce), hamburger, green beans, Tater Tots, and chocolate milk; the long winter sieges through which she wore a worn winter coat because I outgrew mine and needed a new one each year. Or how many lunches she had to miss (or times she had to walk home instead of take the bus) to buy the baseball glove I was convinced would make me a major leaguer (or at any rate, a Chicago Cub).

Years later, she laughed off my admiration.

"I guess some days I'd miss lunch," she said. "And some days some guy would want to take me to Chez Paul's."

(And she'd bring home a doggie bag to share.)

I wouldn't say our lives were always a laugh a minute. But I'll bet two days never passed during which my mother and I didn't laugh loud and long about something that we would find funnier than anyone else.

For my fourteenth birthday, my mother took me to Eli Schulman's place. Not his Oak Street deli, the setting for some of the most cherished late nights of my childhood (my father would fish me from bed to sit on his lap with a company of other comics, who swapped stories, gorged on the buckets of free half-sour pickles that Eli set out—like floral arrangements—on the table, and sipped black coffee as they tried to hold back from scotch), but Eli's steak place a few blocks south. It was a watering hole for athletes, celebs, and pols who liked to **see their names in bold letters** in tabloid columns the next day.

Eli Schulman glittered and winked sporting a dimpled smile and a paisley dinner jacket over a ruffled shirt.

"Patti, honey!" he beamed, for over the years he had seen my mother in his restaurant on a number of arms.

"Eli, I believe you know my son, Scotty. Today is his fourteenth birthday."

Eli had a son the very same age. His face broke wide with delight.

"What a great occasion," he declared. "We'll take good care of you."

He took us to a banquette facing out, the kind they might hold for Frank Sinatra and Ava Gardner. Jimmy, the headwaiter, dashed over to mix a Caesar salad, a peppermill the size of a baseball bat under his arm. He rubbed a garlic clove over the sides of a real wooden bowl as if he were polishing the Stanley Cup trophy.

Our waiter, Harry Briggs, remembered both my mother and father from happy times.

"I remember the night you were born," said Harry. "Your dad said, 'Harry, I don't know if he's gonna make it. He looks so small.'" (I was born two months prematurely.) "And I said, 'He'll make it, Ernie. He knows he'll have a great mom,' and your dad just laughed and laughed. We joshed a lot."

Norb, behind the bar, remembered how my mother liked her Rob Roy. He plunged a skewer of maraschino cherries into my Coke.

Eli brought over Shrimp Marc (shrimp chilled in sour cream, mayonnaise, onions), an appetizer named for his son. No cauliflower tonight! Bring on plump shellfish, pungent garlic, and juicy red meat!

Harry brought over a heavy plate, still glistening and smoking with charred green peppers and onions.

"You like liver, Scotty?"

I made a face.

"You'll like this. House specialty. Extra crispy, so it doesn't taste like liver," and indeed the liver became my favorite dish at Eli's until the day it closed.

The strip steak shimmered. The baked potato crackled on being slashed to receive pillows of butter, swirls of sour cream, and a few shavings of chives (to provide a valuable portion of vegetable nutrition). Eli himself presented a slice of birthday cheesecake only slightly smaller than Michigan's Upper Peninsula. The flames of fourteen candles danced like some fiery line of showgirls.

Eli, Jimmy, and Harry sang.

The bill was presented on a gleaming tray, and when Harry turned away, I saw my mother gulp.

"Darling, do you have any cash?" she asked quietly.

I carried just enough in my pocket for bus fare, a Suzy Q, and the *Sun-Times*.

"I guess I haven't been here in a while," said my mother. "I miscalculated."

"Auntie Chris gave me a card," I remembered. It was in the pocket of my sport coat, and we opened it as anxiously as a note from the Harvard admissions office. Auntie Chris had folded a ten-dollar bill inside.

We had enough to pay the bill and tip the hat-check girl, but nothing left for Jimmy, Harry, and Norb.

"Norb has something in the blender," my mother noticed. "Jimmy is seating a couple in the back. When you see Harry go through the kitchen door for an order, let's make a break for it."

We saw the swinging doors swish behind Harry, bearing a long tray below his arm, and made our move.

The lake wind whipped up the collars of our coats once we got outside on Chicago Avenue, laughing.

"I was going to stop for hot chocolate at the Drake," said my mother. "When I thought we'd have a few dollars left."

"Some other time."

"Jimmy, Harry, and Norb are such lovely people," she said. "And they worked so hard to give you a nice birthday, didn't they? I feel terrible. I'll cash a check tomorrow and stop by with something. They work so hard. They're probably mad at me."

We crossed onto Michigan Avenue to turn north and walk home. No cab—not even a bus—on a night we had to make a break from a swanky restaurant.

"It's a night to remember, isn't it?" my mother laughed. "You can tell people, 'My mother took me to Eli's for my birthday, but had to borrow money from me so we could sneak out.'"

"Guess I won't be able to take the El to school tomorrow."

"I have a little cash in a dresser drawer."

"But I won't have enough cash to buy drugs in the schoolyard," I told her, and my mother gasped and laughed.

"We had a lovely dinner," she said. "Didn't we? And now a wonderful story."

She did go back the next afternoon, and years later, when I went to Eli's as an adult, they remembered that my mother had stopped by with envelopes the next day, which they refused; but she insisted. My mother knew what it was to live on tips, and thought they revealed a person's character. "It's something you do when no one you know is looking."

Eli's (and Eli) have been gone awhile. But the intensive care unit happened to overlook the spot on which it stood, which is now a wing of the children's hospital. Shortly after the palliative care team had trooped softly away, there was another whoosh of my mother's door.

"There's a man at the desk with cheesecake. For *everyone,*" said a nurse. "He says he knows you."

Marc Schulman, the son for whom Shrimp Marc was named, his wife, and their daughters are good friends of ours. Marc had turned his father's classic old Chicago cheesecake into a civic pillar: The mayor of Chicago famously sends Eli's cheesecakes, rather than dead fish. Eli's cheesecakes have nourished inauguration balls. If all the cheesecakes Marc has donated to schools, churches, charities, libraries, ballet companies, and theater groups were laid end to end . . .

And now he'd brought cheesecake to the nurses on my mother's floor.

My mother felt unwashed and unlovely. She'd told me that she didn't want to see anyone. But now she said, "That's Marc. Such a lovely man. I can't let him go without saying thank you."

I brought Marc into her room. Curly hair, a summer shirt, hands so immaculate they made me wonder if cheesecake might be some kind of emollient.

My mother squiggled slightly to sit a little higher on her pillows.

"You look beautiful, Pat," Marc told her, with conviction.

"Oh, you're so kind to say that, Marc."

I think a blush rose through all the tubes to brighten my mother's face.

We talked about family. My mother had a story about Marc's

father, and Marc had one about my stepfather. He told us the latest about his beautiful and accomplished daughters.

After Marc departed, I pulled a chair closer to my mother's bed.

"You should see what Marc brought for the nurses," I told her. "Salted caramel cheesecake. Vietnamese cinnamon cheesecake. And did I tell you? He invited Elise and Lina"—our daughters— "to visit his bakery."

"Such a lovely man," she repeated. "And always so thoughtful. Well, his father was a lovely man, too. Remember all the good times we had at his deli?"

"I remember the tubs of pickles," I told her. "I remember all the jokes with my father. I remember you introducing me to Marshall Caifano"—a local mobster with whom my mother had had a couple of dates—"while he was eating cheesecake all alone, and my eyes popped out of my head. I remember my fourteenth birthday."

My mother laughed about that night all over again until she coughed.

"All the worrying you do about children," she said. "Boys especially. And you boys turned out just fine."

"Do you know they sell Eli's cheesecake in New York and California now?"

My mother shook her head as soon as I began the sentence.

"I don't mean any of that," she said. "I mean the way you've both made such beautiful families."

I tightened my fingers slightly around her hand and my mother closed her eyes.

"Try to sleep," I said softly, and after a moment my mother lifted an eyelid.

"Who's on now?" she asked.

"Rosemary, I think her name is."

"Do I know her?"

"You were asleep when they changed shifts."

"We're sure about to meet now," said my mother. "I have to use a bedpan."

I just want to say that ICU nurses are remarkable people. Thank you for what you do for our loved ones.

8

Listening to La Boheme now, Bocelli. Mother can't keep eyes closed. "Maybe opera will help. I always slept when I went."

I had a few errands to run. I was just about out of clean clothes and the ICU didn't take in laundry. I could also use a little fresh air and sunny streets. So I turned onto Michigan Avenue and saw some of the places where my mother had worked up and down the avenue.

There was the white façade of Water Tower Place, where she had sold English sportswear and learned that "the only people who don't gripe about paying full retail price are gay men." There was the site of the old I. Magnin Building, where she had been the "barn boss" of the Fine Apparel Salon and counseled so many young people in their first or second jobs on their third or fourth romances. There were the ground-floor cosmetics and fragrance counters, sparkling with lights, mirrors, and glass, and heady with the scents of bergamot, sandalwood, and vetiver, where she strolled for exercise and entertainment in recent years, passing the time with young women only recently arrived from

Kraków or Sarajevo. They called her "that nice, elegant lady," kept little giveaway tinfoils of creams and scents for her behind the counter, and told her their stories.

There was a store I'd seen for years but never entered. It had racks of things in fleece and poly-fiber, festooned with placard photos of men and women climbing, scaling, skiing, and spelunking. A salesman approached, hands folded.

I told him, "All I know about the outdoors is that I loathe them."

The young man was unruffled.

"Then perhaps I can direct you to Bloomingdale's, sir?"

He put perfect comic pauses between his words.

"You're too funny to be working in an outdoors shop."

"Actually, I do a little improv on the side."

"I can tell," I told him. "I could use a small mat thingy to sleep on."

"We have a range of small mat thingies," he said. "What kind of sleeping bag thingy do you have?"

"No thingy whatsoever. Just a lot of pillows and blankets."

The man mulled over this a moment and walked me to a case in which small mat thingies seemed to be rolled up flat, glimmering in international emergency orange.

"I don't travel with a bicycle pump."

"Oh, no need," he explained. "People bring these to climb mountains. It takes just a few breaths. All you have to do is blow into this three or four times until it gets firm. Or . . ." He caught my eye. "Or . . . until it says, 'I love you.'"

"Sold," I told him. "Your relentless high-pressure sales technique."

As he ran my credit card through he asked, "So, are we climbing Everest this summer?"

"Couldn't get a reservation. Actually," I told him, "my mother's in the hospital a few blocks away. I've been sleeping on the floor next to her."

When he held the slip against the counter to be signed, it was for a few dollars lower than what was marked.

"You laughed at my jokes," he explained. "Good luck on the floor."

I bought a couple of shirts a few shops away, pleased to find them on sale (remembering my mother's fashion commandment too late: "There's usually a reason something's on sale"). My eyes were dry by the time I came back to my mother's room in the ICU.

"Lookee," I told her, unfurling the mat. The whole head-to-toes of it glowed against the gray floor.

"Hermès orange!" she exclaimed. "Very chic."

A couple of nurses walked in, drawn to the mat like mosquitoes to a campfire.

"I'm not sure we have a blanket good enough for that," said one nurse. "It would be a shame to cover that up."

"You're gonna sleep on that, you'll need Coppertone," said the other.

I picked up a corner and began to blow, as the young man had advised. One, two, three . . . it was stiff by the seventh or eighth.

"A very funny man sold it to me," I told my mother. "I said, 'All I know about the outdoors is that I loathe them,' and he said, 'Then may I direct you to Bloomingdale's, sir?' And when I asked if this was hard to blow up he said, 'Blow into it just a few times until it gets stiff. Or until it says I love you.'"

My mother awarded me a giggle.

"A funny young man. He thanked me for laughing at his jokes."

"There is no great performance without a great audience," said my mother. "Your father taught me that. 'Listen and react,' he used to say. 'Don't wait to make a joke. Just pay attention.'"

"Dad told me that, too."

"It got hard for him," said my mother. "Drinking destroyed his timing. He never slurred his speech. But booze wrecked his listening. It made him hear things. And miss things. He only listened for a way to get to his next drink."

It was something I'd never heard, about a matter my mother and I had worked over about a million times. But now her words sounded conclusive and unqualified. She spoke with the matchless authority of experience and the imminence of death. She didn't need to spare herself any feeling. All would soon be forgiven—she had already forgiven all others—in just the moment of a last breath. If there's anything good to be said for death, it's this final, unsurpassed wisdom, only won through life, which we can hope to have at the end.

I tossed pillows on my mat and pulled over a chair to take my mother's hand.

"Dad always thought you were the funniest person in the world," I told her. "Me too. Whenever I say something mildly, purportedly amusing, people say, 'That's your dad coming out.' But I always knew—Dad always told me—it was you."

My mother screwed up her nose, as if she'd heard a joke that misfired, and then a tube fell out. I sprang forward again.

"Nobody used to tell me I was funny until I met him," she said as she tried to push back the tube with her fingertips. "Your father made me laugh. But truth is, he made me feel funny, too. It's a nice feeling."

My mother closed her eyes and put back her head and sank into sleep within a few breaths. I held on to her hand a few minutes longer, then kissed her fingers and sat back in front of the sunlight coming in the window.

When she went into the hospital for a blood test, my mother had brought along a copy of a book by a friend to keep her company. Wen Huang's *The Little Red Guard* is the story of Wen's family, especially during the turbulence of China's Cultural Revolution. He lives in Chicago now, where he writes beautifully, and is god-father to one of our daughters.

"Wen is such a lovely writer," my mother repeated, time and again, as she read passages from the book. "And to think, he just learned English, didn't he?" (It has actually been twenty years since Wen learned English, a language in which he writes more gracefully than most of us born in Midwestern America.)

Reading had become a struggle for my mother. It was hard to wear her glasses over the oxygen tubing (it was the one irritation she could do something about) and it was difficult to concentrate amid all the beeping, blaring, and disquietude.

I told Wen of my mother's compliment in a brief message. She had been asleep for several breaths when I looked up and saw the author in our doorway. He put a finger to his lips.

"You go downstairs and take a break," he told me.

I recognized a woman in front of me in the line downstairs. She was part of a family that had struggled to sleep on hard, bright pink couches under howling yellow lights in the waiting area. When I stumbled out to the bathroom or elevator, we'd say hello. The grandmother of their family was three rooms down from my mother in the ICU and she was doing not much better than was my mother. The woman's children wailed and fussed. They were worried, hungry, and cranky. I'd stop just long enough to make them giggle with a goofy face, which, a lot of parents will remind you, only inflames kids' spirits after you are safely away.

The woman had a receipt from a beverage that she'd bought a few hours ago, which entitled her to a free drink. But it was hard to tell time in the unvarying hours of the ICU, and although the streets outside were beginning to brighten in the dawn, we hadn't seen the sun.

"This slip is expired," the man behind the counter told her.

I stepped forward.

"Let me buy you a cup of coffee."

She shook her head.

"I miss my children," I told her. "Thank you for letting me fool around with yours. Surely that's good for a cup of coffee."

The small joke had opened a crack in her resolve and she smiled.

"Well, if that's okay."

"What about a cookie, too? Are your kids still here?"

She shook her head again.

"They're with my sister. We couldn't keep sleeping here, all of us."

"I know. I hear their cookies are good."

"Well, okay," the woman said, and when I handed over my card to the man behind the counter he shook his head.

I remembered some lines by Edna St. Vincent Millay that had stopped my mother once as she paged through one of my grade school books.

"What an utterly lovely poem," she'd said. "It's for anyone who's worked the night shift. It's for anyone who's been up with a sick child. This is for anyone who's stayed up all night because they're in love," and as I recalled the verse now I decided that the long night into daylight had been a little bit of all of those for me.

And the sky went wan and the wind came cold,
And the sun rose dripping, a bucketful of gold.

We were very tired, we were very merry,
We had gone back and forth all night on the ferry.

I came back to my mother's room, where an author's reading was in session.

"Oh, dear, Wen has written such a lovely book."

She held his hand.

"And he reads so beautifully. His grandmother! What an amazing woman she was."

Wen had to be on his way, and I walked him to the elevator.

"How does she seem to you?"

"She's in the hospital, Scott," Wen reminded me. "So she's sick. She seems tired. But still so beautiful."

"Did she say anything to you?" I pressed. "Don't violate any confidences. But I think she doesn't want to let me know how she really feels."

Wen drew in his chin and paused to think that over.

"Well, maybe," he decided. "She told me that you talk too much about your children."

Tried to buy coffee for family w/ a mother in ICU too. Barista overheard, refused my card. "Your money's no good here."

9

Our friend Wen Huang dropped by ICU to read to my mother from his book. She smiles, "Haven't we had a lovely day?"

My mother was beautiful. I'd heard it all my life, even though it can be hard for a son to see quite what all the excitement is about over a lady who used to bathe him in a sink.

I could see she had large, dewy brown eyes, and brown-black, almost mahogany hair. Her eyes fluttered, almost like a cartoon character's, with whimsy, kindness, and, you could also see, some of the impishness of a pretty young thing who knew she could get away with a little more than the rest of us.

My mother knew her mix of prettiness and funniness was her calling card. She had weekly beauty shop appointments to keep her hair darker than mine ("I've gone from looking like your younger brother," I told her around the time of her third marriage, "to looking like your older one") and then a couple of fabulous wigs after cancer treatments and age had thinned her hair. But she didn't get nipped, tucked, or lifted.

"Who can afford it?" she'd remark. "Besides, it makes people look like they're always going down a roller coaster."

She'd mention a few names of people we knew who had gotten on that roller coaster, then just as quickly add, "Of course they look fabulous. But . . ."

"You know what is hard?" she said to me now in her room at the hospital. "There's a tone in their voice when you get old and people call you 'lovely.' Like you've become some kind of beautiful, crumbling old statue. They never see you as the person you were before you got trapped in this old body."

My mother shivered and made a face.

My mother had three husbands, a couple more fiancés who I recall hearing about, and boyfriends, dates, escorts, suitors, flames, and swains whom it would be impolite (and possibly impossible) to number. My parents divorced when I was six. So for most of my boyhood my mother was unmarried, pretty, funny, and popular.

After I got old enough to be on my own in our apartment when she went out for the night, she'd leave me with a kind of call sheet for what to tell each so-and-so who called:

> *Earl: I had to work late.*
> (And maybe she did—before she went out.)
> *Jack: I'm with Auntie Chris.*
> (And two ad execs in town for the auto show.)
> *Bernie: There's a new production of* Fiddler *everyone in the office wants to see. . . .*
> (True. But who said they're there tonight?)

The lines she dashed off on a legal pad were convincingly scripted enough (really, Richard Nixon's speechwriters couldn't have been more deft to fall just short of lies). When I was thirteen or so, and became the first adolescent in history to discover adult hypocrisy, I resented my mother's contrivances. Today I see her small fictions as civil, felicitous ways to tell a man, "None of your business."

"We knew some lovely men, didn't we?" my mother said. "Simply *lovely*."

As an adolescent, I was often irritated by the way my mother sprinkled that word, like a favorite seasoning, over every name we mentioned.

"That's so hypocritical!" I'd fume. "That's why my generation can't trust anything your generation says. I bet you'd call Al Capone a lovely man!"

"A lot of people liked him," she reminded me. "He opened food banks. He was nice to his goddaughters."

"See! See!"

But now I was grown—I think I could finally say that—and only moved my chair and took my mother's hand.

"We sure did," I told her. "Lovely guys."

So now my mother and I traded names back and forth. Each set off a small waterfall of recollections.

"Remember Bert?" she began. A mild man, an investment counselor with beige lips and pale hands who wore loud-checked shirts under gray sweater-vests. My mother told him my favorite school subject was current events, so Bert would tuck a small stack of index cards on his knee, just below the table, and sneak surreptitious looks before clearing his throat.

"You know, Scotty," he'd begin, "I read a very interesting article in the *New York Times* the other day. . . ."

"You'd say, 'Oh, it was in the *Tribune* last month,' and make poor Bert feel like an idiot."

"I was the idiot."

"You were young. He understood."

"Then there was Bill."

My mother tightened her lips a little. Bill was an accountant with wavy swells of tawny hair, that my mother seemed relieved to meet because, "He's a nice, normal guy who thinks the most exciting thing in the world is his little blue convertible." They were engaged for a weekend. Bill concocted a scheme whereby we drove out (the top of Bill's blue Chevy was down, and a chorus of gnats flew into our teeth) to his leafy suburban former home to meet his ex-wife, who, he informed us, was such an epochal shrew we could only truly understand him after meeting her.

But Bill had told his ex-wife that my mother was a New York actress who had become his client. I was her son by her famous former husband, who was such a celebrated lout and roustabout it would mortify my mother to so much as breathe a mention of his name.

(But I told myself, "Richard Burton," and hummed a few bars from *Camelot*.)

My mother was then a secretary at an ad agency, and modeled at trade shows. But that afternoon in a suburban backyard, she gave a gold statue performance, enunciating her lines like some lost Barrymore.

"'Oh serpent heart, hid with a flowering face!'" she recited—from high school. "'Deny thy father and refuse thy name!'"

The accountant's ex was delighted and deeply moved. She even began to recognize my mother from some of her greatest roles.

"Beatrice, Viola. I'd say they're my favorites," my mother told her, without, of course, quite adding, *Although I haven't read them since I was a teenager, in summer stock dinner theater and waiting tables.*

"Juliet's nurse has the best lines. I do hope that someday some director will see me that way."

"Who's been your favorite leading man?" Bill's ex-wife asked, and my mother looked reflective.

"Really, I couldn't say."

"Brando? Anthony Quinn? What about—what's his name?—Christopher Plummer?"

"All lovely gentlemen," my mother demurred, blushing with modesty.

The woman Bill had portrayed a shrew turned out to be a gracious host. My mother squirmed to deceive her (and, no doubt, to contemplate living until-death-do-us-part with the man who concocted such a ruse). We got home, I was sent to bed, and heard muffled voices in our living room. The front door of our small apartment closed hard. My mother came to lie down beside me and rub the back of my head.

"I don't think we'll see Bill anytime soon," she said, and in her sigh and the silence that followed I finally heard that my mother was lonely.

"I'd run into Bill now and then," she said now from her bed. "Happy. Turned out fine. Married a lovely gal."

"Did he introduce his wife to Vivien Leigh when she met you? Or whoever you were supposed to be."

My mother snorted through her oxygen tubes. I dabbed some drips. We'd both seemed to hit upon the same name at once.

"Evan?" she asked.

He ran a plumbing company and sent my mother poems written in his own hand. The ones she showed me looked (and I hope this doesn't insult plumbing executives) surprisingly good. One went (it was easy for me to recall):

> Under the summer roses
> When the hot red
> Sleeps in the dusk
> Of the plump red leaves,
> Love, with tiny hands,
> Comes and touches you

He'd signed below, "My deepest thoughts for you. Love, Ev."

"That's a Carl Sandburg poem," my mother laughed when she first showed me what Evan had slipped into the envelope. "Or at least Evan's impression of a Sandburg poem. He's changed a few words. But just a few." She laughed. "Does he think a girl growing up in Chicago doesn't know Carl Sandburg?"

She knew. When my mother was twenty, and worked in Rush Street clubs at night and temp jobs in the Loop during the day, she spent a couple of weeks as the pretty smile installed at the front desk of a law firm. One winter afternoon an elderly man in a battered coat shambled in. "I thought he'd come in from one of the missions downtown," she said. "Where they made guys sing 'Praise Jesus!' and passed out black coffee." The man asked my mother to ring one of the lawyers to say, "Mr. Carl Sandburg is here." She'd turned around to a file cabinet when she felt a hand on her rump. Then a squeeze. She swiveled to see the great, gray poet laureate of Illinois, grinning. "Like a pimply little teen-ager," she recalled. Carl Sandburg was then seventy years old. *Verse-Maker, Stacker-of-Rhymes, Rump-Squeezer to the Nation!*

Evan filched from some other true masters, as I recall: Pound, Shakespeare, e. e. cummings. But my mother soon tired of the game of trying to guess which sonneteer Evan had tried to appropriate. She'd quickly run an eye over his stanzas of endearment and set them aside, like (I'm afraid it's exactly the right analogy) one more unsolicited appeal from a local public radio station.

"Really," she said now from her hospital bed, "he would have gotten farther with me if he had just fixed our shower."

We chuckled like thieves, and when we stopped to catch our breath, I went on more softly.

"And then there was Dr. K."

"A thoroughly lovely man," she said.

"Thoroughly," I agreed.

By the seventh grade, my mother had given me the one bedroom of our small apartment. It afforded me the privacy to do homework, tell dirty jokes to friends on the phone, listen to the music of my generation, and, as I can see now, gave me the isolated habitat an adolescent can use to discover the fruits of puberty without monopolizing the bathroom. *Ahhhem* . . .

(My mother had found a splotch in my sheets one morning and asked, "What's that?" When she could see my face redden like a stove coil, she answered for us both. "Must be coffee," she decided. "Coffee," I agreed.)

My mother slept on a roll-out sofa bed in the living room; it was the kind of sacrifice a mother makes. But it also gave her the limited solitude, in a small apartment, to stay up later and watch Johnny Carson or a late movie of her generation, tell dirty jokes to her friends, and, when she presumed me to be asleep, entertain a friend. Mostly, I really was asleep, and my mother really was watching Johnny. But one night I got up to use the bathroom, cast a look as I rounded a corner into the hallway, and by the dim, fluttering bluish light of Johnny and Bill Cosby or Joan Rivers, I saw the half-moon of a man's bald head and the full moon of his bare bottom.

I recognized the back of that bald head. It was Dr. K, my eye doctor.

I didn't know what I was seeing—but I knew that I shouldn't see it. I crept back into my bed like a cat burglar. I felt my face burn and my heart race. I liked Dr. K, who was quiet, kind, and slyly funny. He wore dapper suits, even as he put drops in your eyes. He had piles of *Architectural Digest,* not just *National Geographic,* in his waiting room. When we came for appointments, I could see that he made my mother laugh. Dr. K had two slightly older daughters, with whom we had once gone to see an ice show. But I sensed nothing going on when the house lights dimmed. Dr. K was an older man, and it was as surprising to see him (especially so much of him) in our living room as it would be to see the cardinal of Chicago.

(More surprising, come to think of it.)

And: I still needed to go to the bathroom. I began to tremble. I considered opening the window in my room just wide enough, but knew it made a rusty, wrenching sound that would only bring my mother racing into the room. I looked for open corners of the closet. But they were already jammed with muddy shoes, old magazines, and spattered baseball caps. I looked at the grill of the radiator cover.

Finally, I spied relief. My mother had given me a pewter mug for my birthday, to mark my interest in writing. I used it to hold pencils. Seeing the mug as I jiggled with discomfort made me exult like a long-haul truck driver who'd been swigging coffee for a hundred miles and just glimpsed a GAS–FOOD–RESTROOM sign. *Relief is just ahead!* I upended the pencils. I inspected the bottom of the mug and determined that it would withstand what I was about to ask of it. I lowered my pajama bottoms, and when

I was done, I slid the pewter mug (warm to the touch, incidentally) below my bed.

My mother found the full mug the next morning, as I was getting ready for school. She was incredulous, fuming, and furious.

"Is this what you think of the gifts that I give you?" she demanded. "Why would you do something so . . ." She struggled for words sharp enough to pierce, and found two. ". . . *sick* and *destructive*." The same words she'd use to describe my father's drinking when she was furious at him.

"I couldn't go to the bathroom," I finally told her, and my mother stood still.

"What do you mean?" she said quietly.

"I mean last night. Around midnight. I couldn't go to the bathroom."

As I run the exchange through my memory now, I wish I had come up with a line as chivalrous as "Must be coffee," or one of the thousand other circumlocutions that my mother had ever minted to keep me from humiliation. Her face froze and then lightened; she turned around wordlessly. Within seconds, I heard plates clink in the kitchen. I picked up the pewter mug from the floor, brought it to the bathroom, and washed it out with tile cleaner. The coffee percolator gurgled, the toaster went boing!, and by mutual agreement my mother and I made the morning normal. Wordlessly, we kept each other's secrets. We were mother and son. We knew where to hurt each other and how to protect each other.

I didn't see Dr. K again until my annual checkup.

(The pewter mug, now dry, sits on a bookshelf at home and holds pencils for our daughters. When they read this, I hope it makes them go, "Eeew . . .")

"Earl?" my mother asked.

"One of my favorites."

"Mine, too. I knew you liked him."

Earl was a large, merry man; a lounge singer who performed under the name "Fat Daddy."

"Nobody loves a fat man," he crooned in his signature song, "but oh how a fat man can love. . . ."

Between gigs that wound through roadside clubs in Wisconsin and Michigan resort towns, Earl lived in a back room of his parents' apartment, keeping a framed photo of Marilyn Monroe on red velvet above his bed, the way I had a poster of the Cubs or Cesar Chavez above mine.

"It's the real deal," he'd tell me with a wink. "I have a buddy, works for *Playboy*. Someday, I'll show you the ones I can't show your mother."

Earl knew that interstate roadhouses outside Kenosha and Buffalo Springs weren't the Sunset Strip. But he loved singing, joking with the band, closing down the bar, and playing golf during the day. "It sure beats working," he liked to say with a wink, though it seemed to me that Earl worked constantly, and was forever in motion. I'd come home from school and our small steel mailbox would spring open when I turned the key, spilling dozens of cards Earl had bought in a sweep of the Hallmark rack at some Waukesha, Waterville, or Oconomowoc drugstore.

The bumper crops of cards made my mother laugh at first. But as the months went on, she began to open them a little wearily, and then began to farm out the chore to me.

"Did you know?" I asked my mother in her bed now. "Sometimes I'd keep the card, cross out Earl's name, write something obscene, and give it to one of my friends."

"Well, I'm glad someone enjoyed them."

My mother fought off a wave of pain and weariness and pulled out another name.

"Jack?"

A sad-looking, hound-faced man with round brown glasses who, my mother imprecisely explained years later, had been supplanted by his younger brothers in an organized crime family (think: Fredo, the sad-sack Corleone in *The Godfather*) and spent most days in his apartment, playing board games, cursing his brothers, and counting the minutes to his first martini. (He didn't count long.) My mother felt sorry for Jack. She agreed to have a drink with him after he sent a three-piece mariachi band to greet her when she arrived for work at one of her jobs (as secretary at *Surplus Record* magazine, which, even in this day of the World Wide Web, is still in business at the same address) in the Civic Opera House.

"I couldn't even tell what they were playing," she recalled. "And I wondered: Do you tip them? In a restaurant, you'd give them something, wouldn't you?"

Jack convinced my mother to have dinner. She insisted that I had to join them. Jack arranged the dinner for his apartment, and set a card table in another room for me and another little boy, close to my age, who was the son of one of the guys in his entourage who ran errands (I assume such errands were benign, or Jack might have had more success in the family business). We had hamburgers and fries—I imagined Jack barking, "Kids! Hamburgers! Fries!"—and mariachis were there, too, playing the Mickey Mouse song over and over, even as the other kid and I agreed we were too mature for Mickey.

Jack soon moved to a Palm something in Florida or California. A local drugstore delivered a bottle of Chanel No. 5 the size of a milk jug to my mother every Christmas Eve, with a card from Jack.

"Did you even like Chanel Number Five?" I asked her now, and my mother squinted.

"It didn't matter, did it? It was a lovely thing to do."

(A few years ago, an elderly man, red-nosed and unsteady, but towering with still-strapping arms, stopped me on the street.

"Bill," he said. "Billy Bananas, I used to go by. You won't remember me."

"You'd think I'd remember a man named Bananas."

"Awww, we barely met. You were a kid. I worked for Jack when your mother used to go with him."

"I think I do remember you," I told him—and I did—and his red face brightened, then sprang a few tears.

"Your mom was a classy lady," he said. "Remember that, kid, whatever you hear. Your ma was a class act. She weren't no whore. Your ma weren't no whore."

That night I told my mother what Bill had said, word for word, and heard a long silence over the line.

"Well, what a sweet thing for Bill to say!" she said finally.)

"I wound up liking Leo," I told her when another name snapped into mind. Leo was an older man who ran a plant on the South Side, collected art in his North Side apartment, and had his shirts done in London (not just made, but *laundered*). He remained devoted to my mother through his divorces and her remarriages, and now and then, in later years, I'd find a card—folded into a book she lent me, or a file of her papers—that he'd written. I read them without telling her, and was touched to see such raw feeling from a man who sent his laundry across the ocean to be starched.

She had gotten one such note on the night before her second wedding. Leo's elegant script looped across a sheet of notebook paper. My mother showed it to me a few years ago, as she sorted through photos and cards. Leo had written,

> *I want for you many things— But the most important is happiness. This you richly deserve— My feelings have not changed nor do I expect they will. As your life goes forwards—if there should be faltering steps or a change in direction—I am here. As a knowledgeable soul and a perceptive woman, you are aware of the great love I hold for you.*

When I read *knowledgeable soul,* I knew that Leo had understood my mother much more than I had appreciated at the time.

"He loved you so much," I told her.

"He was lovely to us, wasn't he?"

"He sure loved you," I repeated, and my mother squirmed a bit, in pain and irritation with my observation.

"He loved *us,*" she said firmly. "But he was a fussy little old bachelor, even when he was married. If you asked to borrow his toothpaste, he'd say, 'Don't you know that I get that from Italy?'"

They'd sometimes have dinner in later years, between marriages and illnesses, and when my mother had complimented Leo on a picture she'd seen in his hallway—French nuns in their tall cornettes, stepping across a courtyard in the rain—he'd sent it over to her in a brown paper package, tied up with string.

"It was so thoughtful."

"He loved you."

My mother moved on to another memory.

"Tommy?"

Tommy, the alderman of a ward two districts north of ours, was a convivial man with a wire-brush moustache. So far as I could tell, the alderman had only breakfast dates with my mother.

She took me along a couple times; I didn't see sparks fly over the bagels. But we got good trash service in our apartment building. He rarely spoke about politics in front of me, but once explained, "You can't be a leader unless you go along with the majority," a line so good it marinated for many years before I finally appropriated it for a political novel.

There was another Jack, a traffic court judge, who took the bus downtown because, "I know how many idiots are on the road—by name." And Bernie, a jocular man who ran a candy company, who used to ask, "Why does everyone get excited about Belgian chocolates? If they're so great, why do the Belgians send them over here?"

"Hy," my mother said, and attached his last name when she said it again.

"What a character, wasn't he? Out of a movie," she said.

Hy was a former boxer who'd gone into the lingerie business and had been married to a B-movie actress who had played the virtuous love interest of Gene Autry. He was a bronzed bottle-blond from Beverly Hills, with a deep laugh and a boxer's strut, the first man I ever saw who wore a powder-blue jumpsuit (indeed, to this day, the only one). Hy would swoop into Chicago every few weeks bearing bunches of flowers and boxes of brassieres, negligees, and camisoles in a range of pinks, whites, and black with red satin laces. My mother and some of her gal pals would pop the tops and giggle, searching for their sizes, and drape the intimate apparel over each other's chests like kids playing dress-up.

Hy kept pads of dollar bills, bound by a Beverly Hills bank, in his pocket to dispense as tips. He held the pad out when he approached waiters and doormen, so they couldn't miss the point.

Hy talked about his recent vasectomy with the kind of admiring awe with which other people spoke about the space program.

"Imagine, Scotty," he said over dinner one night. "Mr. Penirschnitzel can go wherever he wants, and if some dame tries to lasso you, you can say, 'Sorry, babe, I only shoot blanks.'"

"Now, Hy," my mother would rush to try to hush him, "we haven't gone over all the 'facts' with Scotty yet."

"Come see Hy when the time comes," he'd tell me. "Come see Hy for the real facts of life."

I could tell that Hy was outrageous. I liked him for that, and the way he made my mother clamp a hand over her mouth to make sure I knew she was shocked, even as she giggled. It seems to me now that my mother and I had reached a similar conclusion: Hy was great fun to see every few weeks. But perhaps only that.

I knew he was on a campaign to persuade my mother of something more, and deduced from this and that remark that she'd been indecisive or coy in discouraging him.

"I've sold bras door to door, baby," he'd say. "Think I haven't had doors slammed in my face? I keep knocking. You'll see," he assured her. "I make gals with A cups feel like they have D cups."

(Which is not exactly the way, say, Charles Boyer might have phrased it, but was Hy's smoothest patter.)

Hy came by to pick up my mother one night and I served him a scotch on the rocks and scampered into my room to show him a new ink pen. When it wouldn't write, I unscrewed the base to squeeze the cartridge and soon there was a splotch on the rug that looked like a crime scene. My mother gave a toe-curling Hitchcockian scream. But Hy laughed and reached for his pad of dollars.

"Five, ten, twenty," he counted out, gave me that pad, and reached for another.

"Hy, don't," said my mother, but he waved her away.

"Are you kidding?" he said. "The kid just saved me thousands of dollars. Marriage, braces, clothes, food, college. I was all set to pop the question, and . . ."

"Hy, don't," my mother laughed.

"Thousands," he repeated, and plunked another pad of dollar bills into my outstretched, inky hand. "Let me say thanks."

I got to keep only the first twenty.

Another time Hy swooped into town and asked my mother to dinner. She explained that she couldn't possibly because she was set to make dinner for my Auntie Chris, her closest friend, and Chris's sister, who'd just arrived from Iowa. They compromised. My mother would have dinner with Hy—as long as Auntie Chris, her sister, and I were included (which, as I see this sentence, doesn't seem much like a compromise).

Hy brought us to the steakhouse in his hotel. When my mother suggested that she and I might split a portion, he said, "Nonsense. He's a growing boy," and I soon had my own sturdy Chicago sirloin, splashing *au jus* in a heavy-lipped plate. He made sure I had my own baked potato, steeped in sour cream and doused with butter.

"Green thingies on top are chives," Hy explained. "Vegetables. Smaller than pebbles," which at that point of my life sounded like the most appealing vegetable possible. I had an ice-cream snowball for dessert, the hot fudge blazed with some kind of liqueur before our eyes. The glossy sauce sizzled under a blue flame.

Hy pressed another pad of dollars into the palm of our waiter, who packed a bag of cookies for me to take home, or at least up to Hy's hotel room, where my mother would permit me to watch the late news, snack on a last cookie or two, and fall asleep. She would have a nightcap or two with Hy downstairs, and then wake me long enough to pull a coat over my pajamas so a cab could bring us home.

As my mother tucked me into Hy's fresh double bed, she put the television control in my hand. Then she left. I ate one cookie before the news, another during, but left the bag open when I heard, "Heeeere's Johnny!"

The Tonight Show was where some of us adolescent boys wanted to live when we grew up. It was a place on the other side of the wall that we strained to overhear before falling asleep, filled with fresh jokes, sharp clothes, urbane banter, and some glitz to fire a few dreams. On any given night, Charo, Joan Rivers, Carl Sagan, Raquel Welch, or Richard Pryor might be on Johnny's couch. George Burns or David Bowie might pop by. I was not going to sleep with a bag full of cookies by my side and Johnny's monologue ahead.

But within minutes, I heard elevator doors open. Muffled voices in the hallway were headed my way. I snapped off the television. I closed the bag of cookies, and hoped my mother wouldn't count. I turned off the bedside lamp and contrived to appear as if I'd been asleep for an hour. I heard Hy open the door and felt my mother's cool hand on my shoulders. I feigned the breath of slumber.

"He's sleeping," she whispered.

"It wouldn't be cricket to wake him," Hy said. "Let him sleep. We'll get another room."

"I can't. He has school tomorrow. I've got work."

"Room service. Breakfast in bed."

"I can't."

"Honey, it's just not cricket to wake him."

I doubt that Hy (or my mother) had ever seen a cricket match. But an accomplished salesman knew how to appeal to a mother's disinclination to wake her child from sleep.

My mother stood up, perhaps to get my coat, the cookies, and my leftovers. I heard clothes rustling, and Hy's voice dropping.

"Honey, tell me I'm your man."

"I have to get home."

More rustling, a little louder. I could imagine my mother trying to push him away. I was half a second from opening my eyes
and springing out of the bed.

"Tell me I'm your man."

But I heard my mother move away, and Hy stayed where she
left him. He was an honorable old boxer. He might try to nudge,
poke, and dance, but he abided by rules.

I dozed in the cab on the way back to our apartment. The siz-
zling white streetlights cast wands of light over our eyes. I caught
her eye as we made a left turn and the windows caught a glimmer of Oak Street Beach.

"So I'm not getting breakfast in bed?"

My mother pushed her purse into my ribs.

"You little bastard!" she laughed. "You were awake the whole
time, weren't you?"

We got back home in time to see the last ten minutes of Johnny.

I also recall two Pauls (one an ad man, one a banker), and Carl,
who ran an apartment hotel on the North Side where Babe Ruth
and the Yankees had stayed (and to which, perhaps in tribute,
no improvements had been made since). No doubt today my
memory has mixed up their names and identifying attributes,
as you might in trying to remember your first-grade classmates.
But I learned something from each of them. If I sound a little
rueful now, it's because I know I was often an unbearable little
bastard to them then. I'd refuse to laugh at their jokes; or worse,
I'd say I'd heard them before.

(Or worse yet, say, "My father tells that one better.")

Even as I grew older and began to grasp how much his drinking had destroyed—for my mother, for him, even for me—I was loyal to my father. The good men who pursued my mother sensed that. There was almost always a moment on the second or third date when the bathroom door would close for my mother to apply a last dab or spritz and her date would clear his throat, jiggle the ice in his glass, unfold his legs, and lean in a little shyly to say softly, "I don't want to be a new dad, Scotty. I just hope we can be pals. . . ."

They were honest, open, and vulnerable. I was a brat.

My mother would scold me for being a thankless little bastard, and she was right. But at least a little of my misbehavior was bred by what I felt of her own doubts that she would let someone else get truly close to her while my father—funny, troubled, sweet, selfish, charming, rash, and drunk—still had a hold on her heart. She wasn't in love with him, but she found it hard to love anyone else. My father had cracked her heart; she couldn't trust how it worked.

She smiled as we batted names back and forth in the ICU, and half-scraps of memories. Like two old comics, we didn't need to reach the punch lines to laugh. My mother smiled at each name.

"Lovely, weren't they?" she asked again. "Just lovely."

"They sure were," I repeated.

I had to grow up and make my own mistakes to understand how all the little items it once seemed so important to hold against the men my mother knew (they told stale jokes; they whistled old music; they had old political ideas) were, after all, inconsequential. Not every man might have been right or good for my mother. But in all the important ways, they were good men. Lovely, even.

There was silence while my mother let her eyes close, and I clasped my hand around her fingers. We heard another barrage of beeps from a chorus of machines. My mother twitched her lips and lifted her hand.

"Maybe there were a couple exceptions," she said.

"Maybe just one," I told her, and my mother laughed hard enough to sneeze out the tubes from her nose.

"See if you can get a nurse, baby," she told me. "When a gal's gotta go . . ."

My mother drifts to sleep listening to Nat's Unforgettable. I keep things light, but moments like this hard, if sweet.

10

I consider this a good sign: mother sez when time comes, obit headline should be Three Jewish Husbands, But No Guilt.

I once met my mother for dinner at a place she'd wanted to try, and realized I didn't know which name she had used to make the reservation.

"Try Simon first," I proposed. "My name. And the name of my mother's first husband."

The hostess shook her head.

"Newman?"

Ralph Newman, her second husband. They were married for twenty-five years. My mother was still Pat Newman to many friends, and kept the name on her medical records, driver's license, and voter's registration card.

The hostess looked down a second time and shook her head. "No Newman either."

"Gelbin?" I finally suggested.

Matthew Gelbin was my mother's third husband. They would be married for eight years.

"Bingo," said the hostess. "I knew that if you kept guessing, you'd finally hit one right."

When my mother joined me, I told the hostess, "And here she is, my mother: Patricia Lyons Simon Newman Gelbin."

"There must be a story behind all those names," said the hostess, and my mother made a little vinegary face.

"I never set out to be a collector," she told her.

My mother always married for love. But each marriage seemed to embody what she'd learned as she went along. She was truly, madly, deeply, and a little crazily in love with my father, Ernie Simon. He was funny, playful, rascally, and kind. They met in the years just after the war (my mother remembered that the buzz of a low-flying plane would make my father duck into a crouch, a reflex left over from serving with the British Army in North Africa). He had kept his clipped David Niven–ish officer's moustache, and was dashing and slim before bourbon and vodka made him bloated and wobbly.

"He was the love of my life," my mother told my wife the night before our wedding. She'd never revealed that to me, in so many words. She wanted to respect Ralph, her second husband, and, I think, my mother had decided that her rapturous love for Ernie Simon had been a little—more than a little—dangerous. It was certainly not the kind of love you'd encourage for your son.

They were married for nine years. My mother used to say that two or three of those years were good. I thought she meant the first two or three years, before drink overtook my father. But now in the ICU she told me, "The drinking was bad from the first. But Ernest was sensitive. He was funny. He was an artist. So he drank. It's easy to fall in love with a drinker. They're charming.

You make them happy. But it's one thing to fall in love with someone who drinks, and another thing to wake up with him, day after day."

"What were the two or three years?" I asked.

"Twenty or thirty days out of a year that your father was utterly delightful. It added up to two or three years out of nine, I'd guess. Enough to keep me going, until I realized that wasn't enough to give a child."

"How did you last even nine years?"

My mother curled her lips to send a burst of her breath skyward.

"There was always something more important. I got pregnant. I thought maybe a baby would change him. But we lost her at birth, and then I didn't want him to bear any more hurt. I didn't want any more hurt, either. Then we went on the run, from city to city, San Francisco to Cleveland and back to Chicago, Ernest always drinking himself out of jobs, trying this or that doctor, group, or cure, then giving up. I couldn't leave him after all that. It would be, 'Et tu, Patti?' Another knife to his heart."

"And that got to nine years."

"I never counted until it was over," my mother said. "Every day, I'd get up and hope it would be like the second or third day we were together."

My father was in decline for most of my life, and while he made me laugh, and I loved him a lot, it made it hard for me to see him as my mother had: sharp, slim, impish, and charming. But every now and then, I got a glimpse.

We were on the run, from city to city, as my mother put it, when we washed up in San Francisco. My father often worked until the wee hours in clubs in North Beach, and would come home to our hotel room just as the sun began to burn through the gauzy swirls of fog outside our windows.

I would bounce out of my mother's bed, and into his arms. He'd smell of Old Spice and Early Times. He'd kiss my slumbering mother on the forehead, and she'd mutter a few words. He'd sink heavily into a chair by the window and unscrew the top of a fresh bottle. It would not last the day. I still hear the first glugs as they splashed into a hotel glass.

"Morning, Ace," he'd say.

"Morning."

We kept a box of cornflakes—or Rice Krispies or Wheaties— on the windowsill, and would sprinkle flakes into our hands.

"I can't believe you boys," my mother would say from under the covers. "Eating cereal like that. My little boys. My little doggies."

My father had to wear his great gray houndstooth overcoat even on summer mornings in San Francisco, and would swoop me into his arms, pull a jacket over my shoulders, and head back outside. There was a movie theater near the wharf that showed nothing but cartoons on Saturday morning. My father would sleep and snore while I laughed at Heckle and Jeckle, Bugs Bunny, and Popeye. The ka-pows and ka-booms sometimes jolted him awake, and he'd shake his head like some cartoon cowbell. He'd stay awake for a few minutes, and whisper his own dialogue for Bugs and Porky, make me laugh, then put his head down on the back of his seat and snooze deeply. I have sometimes wondered if I have worked on Saturday morning for so much of my life as a way to recapture those hours with my father.

We'd stay until the Three Stooges came on, when older kids began to file into the theater, snorting and snickering. There was a shop next to the movie theater that made marzipan candies. There were lipstick-red marzipan apples, sun-yellow marzipan lemons, bold orange Golden Gate bridges, and on the lowest shelf behind the glass, bright brown marzipan dog turds. The candy excreta sparkled with great gleaming flakes of sugar.

My father and I would walk out onto Mason Street, chomping conspicuously.

"Isn't this delicious, Ace?"

"Best ever, Dad!"

The shop had other specialties, including a multihued marzipan pool of vomit. My father bought one on a Saturday and slipped it into the folds of his coat. When we got back to our hotel room, he unwrapped the candy barf in the bathroom and plopped it on the floor just under the toilet.

"Okay, Ace. Run and get Mommy. Like we rehearsed."

"Mommy, Mommy," I called as I scampered through the hall. "Come quick! Daddy is sick!"

My mother came running. She saw my father, bent over next to the toilet, contriving to look green.

"Don't worry, babies," she said in a sweet singsong. "Mommy will clean it up. Both of you boys just lie down—you must be sick. Mommy will take care of this."

I think her sweet concern made my father and me feel (briefly) sheepish. But we had to get on with our act. My father reached down for the marzipan spew, and picked it up with his fingers. Then he took a bite.

My mother screamed. It was a screech from a horror film. It bounced off the bright, white tiles, drilled our ears, made our blood sizzle, and steamed up the windows. And then her scream turned around in her throat and my mother began to laugh. She started to giggle. She laughed so hard she had to sink to her knees. I was four or five years old and I think I realized in that moment that however my father angered, upset, and let down my mother, he could make her laugh—and she could make him laugh—like no one else. I think I even felt a little left out to see the two of them, crying with laughter on the cold, white tiles, in love, un-glued, enchanted, mad, and lost.

My mother didn't marry for the second time until four years af-ter my father died. They had been divorced for twelve, but I came to think that she merely went through the motions of romance with most of the men she met while my father was still alive.

(After all, the motions could be fun.)

She fell hard for one man in that time, and almost went over a cliff. We would talk about that one last time in the ICU. But she found her feet, then found Ralph Newman.

Ralph was a stocky, ebullient man with a cheery red-apple face and a crumpled nose that often made people smile back (his nose had been rearranged by a triple, when he was briefly a minor league ballplayer).

My mother had watched the love of her life drink himself into a nosedive. She found a love with Ralph that was steady and sane. They were good for each other. They had a lot of fun.

Ralph was a jazz fan and a Civil War buff, he ran a lively little bookshop (the Abraham Lincoln Bookshop on Chestnut Street, now leveled to make way for a hotel garage), and was pres-ident of the public library board. He made the shop into a kind of impromptu after-hours club. I remember a night on which a visiting author, a local alderman, a local madam, and a Chrysler dealer sat around Ralph's shop after hours, eating my mother's snacks and telling jokes; all we needed was a rabbi.

Ralph's two daughters from a previous marriage (he also married three times) were grown and out of town. I was in town, but just on my own. So my mother and Ralph could go places. They took Civil War Roundtable trips to the likes of Springfield and New Salem, and jaunts to see Lincoln collectors in Beverly Hills and Tokyo.

People used to wonder how my mother could marry a comedian and then a Lincoln scholar. But my father was a comedian with an eighth-grade education and highbrow aspirations. Ralph Newman was a Lincoln scholar (albeit with just a year of college— "more than Lincoln and Sandburg had, put together," he used to note) with an entertainer's instincts.

Ralph devised a sideline expertise to appraise letters and documents. This brought a number of famous people to his shop when they learned they could pile their old letters and carbon copies into boxes, give them to a school or library, stamped with Ralph's appraisal, and take a tax deduction. Adlai Stevenson and Carl Sandburg were his first famous clients. ("All those famous goddamn poems Carl wrote for just five bucks," Ralph said. "It was only right for him to get a little back from the IRS. Every kid in America learned his poems by heart, for free.") His client list grew to include William O. Douglas, Lyndon Johnson, Leon Uris, Dalton Trumbo, and, in time, Richard Nixon.

And this is where this most steadfast of men got himself into trouble. Ralph was indicted for backdating an appraisal that enabled Richard Nixon to take a tax deduction for his papers (many of which were carbon copies of form letters) after the legal deadline. President Nixon's tax returns were investigated as part of the crimes surrounding Watergate.

It was the kind of indictment prosecutors usually used to pressure a witness to testify against a bigger fish. But by the time Ralph's case came to trial in late 1975, President Gerald Ford had already pardoned his scaly predecessor. Ralph had nothing to trade for his testimony. He went to trial and pleaded no contest.

Many (perhaps most) marriages don't survive a trial and conviction. People have to pay their life's savings to defend themselves; then their careers and reputations are so ruined, whatever the verdict, it's hard to make a living thereafter.

Ralph was defended by two Washington lawyers who slept on sofa beds in the bookshop to save on his expenses. They called one night to tell me and my mother to come over. They had tried an exercise with Ralph where they asked the questions he could expect from prosecutors, should he take the stand; he didn't have good answers.

"We know this can be devastating for a family," they told us. "You realize that the person you love hasn't told you the whole truth. Just remember: he needs you more than ever."

Ralph came into the room slowly, as if trudging through sleet. He flashed a smile, and then seemed to remember what brought us there. His eyes were red as he looked for a place to sit, not sure if it was next to us or across the room.

My mother called out, "My hero." Ralph sat beside her while she lifted his hand and kissed it, and then brushed his cheek.

"I've been thinking, darling," she announced, to the lawyers, to her son, and to Ralph. "I don't want you to go on the stand. Those bastards would just twist your words. Keep your dignity. You're the sweetest man in the world."

My mother was right on all counts.

The sharpest remark I ever heard my mother make about Ralph's crime and conviction in all the years that followed was, "Some gals worry about their husband lying to them about Raquel Welch. Ralph stepped out on me with Richard Nixon."

A lot of Ralph's appraisal clients canceled ("I guess you know you're too hot to handle," said Ralph, "when Spiro Agnew cancels on you"). But an impressive number stayed. Their faith was a tribute to Ralph's essential honesty and gift for friendship.

Against a lot of expectation and experience, my mother and Ralph grew closer through all their trials. But The Troubles, as we came to call them, turned what he'd planned to be a comfortable glide into their declining years into a financial scramble. In time he had to sell his bookshop, and then opened another, which soon failed (losing what my mother considered their household savings, too).

Ralph worked into his mid-eighties. But then his great heart began to break down. He was in and out of hospitals, then sentenced to a wheelchair, and spent hours during what turned out to be his final months sitting up in bed, shutting his eyes, and listening to Louis Armstrong, hour after hour.

"Great music," I'd tell him.

"I close my eyes and I'm back there," he said. "In my twenties. Listening to Louis and King Oliver on the South Side. I can walk. I can run. I'm young enough to come back from any screw-ups."

One night I got ready to leave their apartment and my mother sat on their sofa, listening to Louis in the next room. She tried to thumb through a book of art prints, but her eyes shined; she had to dab them with a kitchen towel.

"When we married," she told me, "I could tell that Ralph loved me a little more than I loved him. But I figured I would grow to love him more, and I did. He was so kind. So funny. So good. And I knew he would be good for you."

"He sure was. I love him."

"But now that we're near the end," she said, "I think we've traded places. I can see that the life he's had with me has been just a short time in a long life. But those twenty-five years mean so much more to me. And now, I don't know how I'm going to go on without him."

I sat down and we watched the small specks of headlights nose up and down the avenues outside.

After Ralph Newman died, my mother became part of a merry and remarkable group of women, all widowed, who lived in her building and kept moving. They explored the city each day, went to plays, movies, museums, galleries, and new restaurants opened in bare storefronts in edgy neighborhoods by adventuresome young chefs using novel ingredients in new ways.

My mother loved the women; so did I. They had fun. But she also thought the bustle and busyness didn't substitute for living in long-term commitment with someone, even if rationally you knew the "long term" was pretty close. The "until death do us part" part seemed like just the next page on the calendar.

My wife and I took my mother to the Goodman Theatre one night, and during intermission I fixed my eye on the donors' wall. The names of generous theatergoers were engraved on small brass plates. I asked the theater's director, "Any widowers up there?"

My mother met Matt Gelbin at a party on New Year's Day, five years after Ralph died, and a few days later Matt told her, "I've been thinking. We should get married."

Matthew was active, spry, and *normal* in a way that was almost novel for my mother. He was a retired furniture executive (three words that, individually or in succession, were hard to imagine attached to my father or Ralph Newman). He had been a volunteer at the Lincoln Park Zoo. He'd had a long, happy marriage to his second wife, who had died of a sudden stroke not long before he met my mother.

Matthew took my mother to the opera (he loved the music; she liked the costumes). He left phone messages—"It's Matt, the new boyfriend . . ."—which my mother played over and over for us, evaluating each word, as if it were an international trade proposal. "What do you think he means?" she asked.

And Matthew was—is—healthy and vigorous. My wife and children and I might swoop in to bring my mother to shows, shopping, on trips, and to chefs' tables. But Matthew was with her when she couldn't stop coughing at four in the morning and cried out for help. Matthew was the man who reminded my mother when to take the pills that multiply with the years, and the one who told her, "You've lost too much weight. See the doctor." Matthew sat by my mother's bed in the ICU for days before I ever showed up.

People marry for different reasons in different seasons of life. My mother married once, when she was young, for a breathless, reckless kind of romantic kamikaze love. Many people keep repeating their mistakes in romance (my mother did a little of that, too), but by the second time she married, it was for a level-headed love that let her catch her breath; and then her love grew. It does Matthew no dishonor to say that he and my mother married for companionship. Simple, daily, caring closeness is often the scarcest, most precious, and delightful missing vital item in the lives of people when they grow older.

"Three husbands!" my mother said in the ICU now. "It makes me sound like some international woman of intrigue. But really, I just outlasted two of them. I guess I finally had to marry a man who'll outlast me."

We heard the squeal of a cart stopping in the hallway followed by the now-familiar whoosh of the sliding door. Anne had returned.

"Are you keeping your mom up all the time?" she asked. "Do I have to send you downstairs for coffee again, so she can get some rest?"

My mother just knitted her fingers into my hand. We wanted to keep going with each other.

Mother can't sleep. We listen to music, her face feels puffy, hot. We talk of much. I say "You need sleep." "Not really."

11

Mother & I just finished a duet of We'll Meet Again. Every word has meaning. Nurse looks in, asks, "Do you take requests?"

The man for whom my mother almost went off a cliff was Phillip Alton Whyte. He was elegant, stately, tanned (which he managed in Chicago, in winter, Max Factor supplementing his glow between trips to Palm Springs), and slightly jowly in a refined, equine way, the appearance of which he tried to offset by wearing an ascot (in Chicago, on an average Thursday).

So of course I called him Ass Face.

Mr. Whyte had an apartment on Astor Street. In that home, he had a wife, who he said had denied him a marriage bed and a divorce, and a son and daughter who were at least a dozen years older than me. He'd show us photos of them, appearing at charity polo matches or cotillions, when they ran in glossy magazines of the kind you might see on the coffee tables of hotel lobbies.

Ass Face.

Mr. Whyte came to our apartment on Thursday nights. He

would change into a robe (powder-blue silk in summer, burgundy wool in winter), because he had a bad back. He would sit down with a scotch, and we'd order in. Mr. Whyte wanted to be a classy gent. So we didn't order in pizza or chow mein, but linguine doused in red sauce and crowned with meatballs, chicken enrobed in squishy Parmesan, and cannoli, squirting cream. There was always enough to stretch into my school lunch for the next day. We talked about what was in the news, and he told stories about his cosmetics business and what seemed to me to be a lot of trips to exotic spots where he'd spend the week on a boat with people whose names were unfamiliar to me but caused my mother to coo, "Really? What's he like?" At around six thirty, Mr. Whyte would push back from the table and say, "You know, Scotty, I hear there's a good movie at the Village . . . ," then reach for his money clip, snap off a ten, and ask, "Would this be enough?"

When I got back in a few hours (the ten was also enough for a late snack at the Village diner, and a musty used paperback from a store on Lincoln Avenue), my mother would be asleep in her roll-out. Two small liqueur glasses, scarcely sipped, would be left standing on the coffee table next to her bed, perfuming the room with brandy.

As I got older, I'd sometimes down what was left in the glasses before depositing them in the kitchen sink, and I'd think, Mr. Whyte's back couldn't really be all that bad, now could it?

They had met when my mother shot a newspaper ad for the hairspray he manufactured. She was the wide-eyed brunette who smiled to see her hairdo stay beauty-shop fresh in the rain (which was actually water dribbled through a screen over her head in a photo studio on the West Side), and he was the president of the company that made bargain-priced hair products.

("The same stuff that's in Lady Clairol," he told me more than once. "Clairol just makes you pay more to think that Audrey Hepburn uses it too.")

He asked my mother to have dinner (I imagine he ended a lot of photo shoots that way), and after she made him laugh, he sorrowfully disclosed the pain of his cold, loveless marriage. I don't know what led to what and when, but Mr. Whyte's Thursday night pajama-and-Parmesan parties began within a few weeks.

He never deceived my mother about being married. He told her (and me too, when I got older and he figured I might need more than a ten-spot and a cannoli to keep his secrets) that his wife would not grant him a divorce without preventing him from seeing his children and divesting him of every cent and stitch.

I spot a few holes as I retell his yarn now. Divorce laws were restrictive in those days, but Mr. Whyte's son and daughter were already just about grown, and I'd wager they'd probably guessed their father didn't really spend Thursday night (and for all I know, many another night) playing cards in a private room with no phone at his gentlemen's club downtown (which was his cover story). I went through some years resenting Ass Face for treating my mother like some especially intimate appliance rolled into service weekly. There was an old history in urban America of blue-chip spoiled sons frolicking with Irish (or Polish, Italian, African-American, Appalachian, Puerto Rican, or Czech) maids, waitresses, and bellhops, who they considered good for bonking, but not wedlock.

This view had cold logic, but no flesh and blood. My mother and Mr. Whyte got the kind of love they wanted from each other. It was reliable, limited, and noncommittal.

(And my mother would probably have had little interest in

marrying a pauperized Phillip Alton Whyte, dressed in a barrel instead of Turnbull & Asser.)

Mr. Whyte was nice to me. I enjoyed his stories, he listened to mine, and although I never saw him outside of our apartment (for that matter, rarely when he wasn't in a robe), we struck up a relationship on the certainty that he was part of our lives for just one night a week. He gave me a beautiful brown briefcase from Marshall Field's when I graduated high school. I returned it the next day because he'd told me, "I'm giving this to you because I know your dad can't," which was true but not kind. A married man can't expect to score points for truth with the son of his mistress.

Thursday nights with Phillip Alton Whyte ran from about the time I was eleven or twelve through my late teens. Sometimes a few Thursdays would go by without him—more, it seemed, as I got older—until one night I got home and heard my mother breathing in great, broken jags. I was alarmed. I snapped on a light. There was a note on yellow paper next to the phone, her rosary, a small Infant of Prague medal, and a little brown bottle that I knew held (because she told me never to take one) sleeping pills. (My mother and her pals passed around a lot of sleeping pills and diet pills in those days.)

I shook the bottle and heard that it was empty. The note my mother wrote went:

So sorry.
I love PAW.
I have only loved PAW.

I leaned over and tried to wake her. She didn't stir, but kept breathing—gasping. I got scared, took her shoulders, and shook hard. My mother whimpered.

"How many did you take?"

Her voice was slow, sluggish, and small.

"I . . . don't . . . know."

"How many?"

"I . . . didn't . . . count."

"I'm calling an ambulance," I told her, and my mother shook her head slowly.

"No . . . no . . . *no*," she said, the last one vehement. "Don't call. . . . Don't . . . please . . ."

I wanted my mother to live and I didn't want her to be humiliated. I already knew that Phillip Alton Whyte took the elevator to a higher floor and walked down to ours, to avoid any deductions a neighbor might make about whom he saw in his timely appearances. An ambulance—the howl of the siren, the loud glare of red light—would oblige making explanations to our neighbors.

But I remembered a name—Eddie, a doctor—from conversations with Phillip. He lived on Lake Shore Drive and was Mr. Whyte's alibi for the card game at his club. Information gave me a number, which rang at an answering service. It was shortly after eleven and I heard an ensemble of voices in a small room.

"The doctor isn't available. Can I take a message?"

"It's an emergency," I told the operator, and heard my voice turn high and tight in my throat.

"Have you called Emergency Services?"

"No," I told her, "because it's a woman who tried to take her life because of her boyfriend, Phillip Alton Whyte, who is the doctor's best friend."

There was a pause while I heard surrounding voices repeat: "The doctor isn't available. . . ."

"And you are?" said the one I was talking to.

"The patient's son."

"And your mother is the doctor's patient?"

"No. But he'll know her name: Patricia Simon. He's been covering up for his best friend for years so he can see her. My mother has swallowed a whole bottle of sleeping pills because of that bastard," I told her in a tumble of words, "and if the doctor doesn't come over and save my mother's life, it's murder."

After a pause she said, "I'll see if I can inform the doctor."

The phone rang within three or four minutes. My mother whimpered at the blare of the bell.

"You must be Scotty," said the doctor. "Do you know how many pills she took?"

"The bottle is empty."

"But she's breathing?"

"Badly."

"Talking? Is she coherent?"

"Are you coherent?" I bellowed. "Do you hear what I'm saying?"

"I'll get a cab," said the doctor. "Don't let her sleep. Talk, shake her, whatever you have to do."

I slammed down the phone and nattered on loudly about nothing. School, sports. I sang Beatles songs. I recited the Gettysburg Address. I delivered Mercutio's Queen Mab speech, over and over. Every minute or so, I'd shake my mother's shoulders.

"Don't . . . please . . . sleep . . ."

"No. *No!*" I told her.

The doctor arrived. He was bald, slightly breathless, and wore a gray golf sweater. He called my mother Patti and opened her eyes with his thumb to shine a penlight into them.

"Good," he said. "Let's get her up. Into the bathroom."

We threaded our arms around my mother's shoulders. She stumbled but still put down her feet, and we brought her to the toilet and set her on her knees. The doctor held her head in his hands and looked over.

"This won't be pretty," he told me.

After about an hour, once my mother had brought up the pills and the doctor had me make black coffee to pour into her, the buzzer by our doorway blared and Eddie, as the doctor now invited me to call him, whispered, "I called Phillip . . ."

"Good," I replied. "Let him see what he's done."

Mr. Whyte had hurried into his clothes. He wore no ascot or tie, and hadn't puffed a pocket square into his blazer. Besides, it would be hard to know how to dress for the occasion.

His finely turned face was grave, his voice low.

"How is she?"

"Like you care, asshole. Bastard. Son of a bitch."

I ended every sentence I directed to Phillip Alton Whyte that night with an epithet. They got worse. I used phrases I'd picked up in schoolyards and locker rooms, and the punch lines of the vilest jokes I'd heard from the crudest jokesters and delinquents in school. I wanted to hurt him. I smiled as he flinched and shrank at each curse. Now and then, he'd try to mollify me, asking, "Do you really think I ever wanted something like this to happen?" But I flung Mr. Whyte's words, almost too easily, back into his face.

"What did you think would happen, dickhead?"

Dr. Eddie had reckoned, from what he'd seen in the bathroom, that my mother had swallowed about a dozen pills, and decreed that we had to keep her on her feet and away from sleep. So we took turns, two by two, holding her up by her shoulders to walk around our small living room. My mother's eyes stayed shut, but she murmured now and then, and her feet shuffled over the floor.

"Stay with us, Mother," I'd say. "Tell us about the time you and Dolores Gonnella saw Billy Eckstine at the Green Mill."

"Hmmm," she murmured. "It . . . was . . . nice."

We snapped on a radio, but the after-midnight music was too soothing. I dialed up a rock station, but Eddie said that music would make my mother gobble more pills. He smiled, and I knew she must have been pulling out of danger. I would help walk my mother for half an hour or so, then sit, then get up to tour the living room again. Now and then Phillip and I would find ourselves joined together around her shoulders, and he'd try to open a conversation.

"I wonder, Scotty, if you've noticed these lads in the city council who are such upstarts—"

"Of course," I'd cut him short. "*Scumbag.*"

At some point that night (I think I'd been saving the word, like the king in a royal flush), I called Mr. Whyte a *motherfucker.* I knew that's what ballplayers called umpires when they really meant business. He flinched again, as if absorbing a blow, but I heard myself say it aloud and cringed. The word was too close.

We could see sun light up the garage roof and backsides of apartment buildings that were our living room view. Dr. Eddie said that my mother could return safely to sleep now.

"You should sleep too," he told me. "All of us, I guess."

"It's good to know our girl is going to be okay," said Mr. Whyte.

"She's my mother. She's not 'our girl.' *Asshole.*"

He sat back. He was unshaved, his forehead slick and shiny, silver hair scraggly, his open collar crumpled. I thought: If your girlfriends could see you now, a horny, fading, middle-aged man.

Mr. Whyte caught his breath as if he'd just climbed a few flights of stairs.

"I can see why you feel that way. It's just that after tonight, I feel like we shared something important together."

"We shared dick. *Son of a bitch.* I just walked in just in time to keep you from killing my mother."

Mr. Whyte sucked in another long breath.

"I can see why you're upset."

"I'm not upset. I just hate you. *Asshole.*"

I felt a flash of pity for Phillip Alton Whyte. A woman he loved and with whom he thought he had a mutual, undemanding understanding had threatened to upend his happiness; now he had to contend with an angry boy who wasn't his own, and whom he couldn't disown or fire.

"Someday," he said softly, "you'll realize how much I really love your mother."

"Go fuck yourself. *To death,*" I told him, and Mr. Whyte's fine gray eyes turned glossy.

Today, I wonder if he was trying to tell me that he had been more instrumental in our lives than my mother wanted me to know. Phillip Alton Whyte, after all, owned a boat, got photographed at charity balls, went to polo matches, and hobnobbed with other names on the donors' plaques of art museums and theaters. Did he ever help pay our rent? Or send me to summer camp? Or on my class trip to New York, to see my first Broadway play, or for the weekend my mother and I saw *Antigone* and *Romeo and Juliet* at the Stratford Festival? Did Ass Face, without my knowing, buy me the typewriter that I wanted or promise to pay for college? Mr. Whyte gave my mother a couple of nice pieces of jewelry (I recall a necklace and a watch). But I never saw her wear them after she married Ralph Newman, and we didn't find them tucked on a closet shelf or in a dresser drawer after she died.

I don't think my mother made a financial arrangement with Phillip Alton Whyte to share each other's company on Thursday nights. But money was one of the few things he was free to share. And I can see how my mother could bring herself to see anything he gave her as a sign of love.

"Every time the phone rings," I told him, "I want you to jump—I want you to have a heart attack—because it might be me, telling your wife what a bastard you are."

"My wife knows. I assure you. We have separate lives. A call like that would only hurt my children."

He swallowed hard and his voice snagged.

"And I hope you won't want to do that."

"And you picked a bad time to ask me for a favor."

I saw Phillip Alton Whyte just a few times after that long night. I moved away, and once or twice when I came home for a week or a weekend he'd be back in my mother's living room, his ascot obstinately knotted, sipping a scotch. We'd chat amiably of nothing for a while and then he'd excuse himself, shaking my hand and leaving what looked like a chaste peck on my mother's cheek before she closed the door.

But his splendid burgundy wool robe reappeared when my mother packed up her closet to move in with Ralph Newman before they married.

"Say, that's a beaut," said Ralph. "Brooks Brothers, too." The Lincoln scholar spied the label. "Whose is it?" I was about twenty and usually wore not much more than blue jeans and a work shirt—the same ones—day after day.

My mother caught my eye.

"It was my dad's," she said. "Remember?"

I tried to imagine my grandfather, the Chicago cop, drawing that burgundy wool robe over his boxer shorts and sleeveless T-shirt at the kitchen table.

"Well then, why don't you take it?" Ralph suggested to me, and so I did. But I could never bring myself to wear it (I wouldn't be so fussy now), and I think I gave it to Vinko, the landlord of a building in which I lived, because he looked the other way when I used the washing machine in the basement after ten o'clock.

Years later, I hovered over the size 16s during the post-holiday sale at a men's store when I caught sight of Mr. Whyte. He was still handsome, elegant, and straight-backed as a rider in a horse show. But he doddered on his feet, and held on to the rails of a walker. He was with a woman, blue-eyed and elegant, dripping with shiny, twinkly things. I took her to be his wife, so I looked away. Not because I was still angry, but because it's what my mother always told me to do if I encountered Phillip in public.

But Mr. Whyte caught my eye and put out his hands. By the time I went over to take his, he was blubbering.

"I've been following this young man," he told his wife. "I like to think that maybe I had a little bit to do with helping him."

"You sure did, Mr. Whyte."

His wife pursed her lips in my direction—I couldn't tell if she was going to smile or spit—and looked away. I didn't know if my name meant nothing to her, if she identified it with my mother, or if over the years Mrs. Phillip Alton Whyte had met a dozen other young men or women who knew her husband in the same way.

The last time I'd put my hands on Mr. Whyte's arms it was to tell him, "I want you to have a heart attack." This time I said, "You were always good to me." I had spent years being angry on my mother's behalf. Now that I was grown up and had a name of my own, I understood that she'd be prouder of me for being gracious.

It was a couple years after that when my mother got a call from Eddie, Mr. Whyte's friend, the doctor who had come out in the middle of the night to help my mother (and to protect Phillip Alton Whyte).

"He's in the hospital," the doctor told her. "It doesn't look good. He's asking for you. I know you're married, happy. It's all past. I'd understand if you didn't. But . . ."

My mother told Ralph, "This was a man I knew before I ever knew you. I never told you about him, though, because he was married and I was embarrassed. I'm not in love with him—I love you—but I want to do what's right. He's asked to see me and I feel that I have to."

And Ralph said, "I'll drive you."

All these memories passed in a moment between my mother and me at just the mention of Mr. Whyte's name. She closed her eyes again, but not completely; which I took as a sign she was open to a question that had lain between us for years.

"What were you trying to do that night?"

I tightened my hand. My mother paused to let a few beeps and buzzes from all the learned machines bleep between us. She waited for a quiet spot to say, "I guess I was desperate. *Desperate*," she repeated. "I told Phillip we couldn't go on. But he kept coming back. And I kept taking him back. I felt I had to do something to remind us that we were playing with fire."

She squeezed her eyes now, as if trying to see something in darkness.

"I figured I'd just throw up a lot, you'd get home and call him. Just once, I wanted his phone to ring at home."

"What if the State Street bus broke down? What if I didn't get home in time?"

"I was ashamed," my mother said finally. "I was willing to let whatever would happen to me happen."

"You loved Mr. Whyte?"

"By now you know that there are different loves."

"You wanted to marry him?" And at this my mother began to move her head from side to side.

"He always told me that he couldn't. He never lied to me. Maybe the longer we went on, the more I hoped that would change. But even if his wife had said, 'Take him,' I realized I wouldn't really want that. His children would shut him out. That would make him hate me. So I'd hate him if he sided with his children, and I'd hate him if he turned his back on them. We could never trust each other and we'd never be happy."

My mother had opened her eyes wide by now. They looked huge, dark, and damp. I brought her hand under my chin as the door opened behind us and a man in a green coat tugged some machine into my mother's room. She looked at me while he snapped on a couple of pale lights, and lowered her voice to bring me forward.

"Phillip knew that too. He wasn't a bastard. He knew you were getting older. He said, 'We can't hide things from him anymore.'"

I spent a while—wasted the time, really—trying to decide if my mother or Phillip Alton Whyte was more to blame for their relationship. But blame for what? They were two consenting adults, experienced runners around the romantic track, who each got what they wanted from each other for a time, and certainly what sophisticated people should expect.

I heard my mother warn a lot of friends against taking up with a married man. She'd tell them (she'd heard it from her mother—maybe all daughters do), "If he'll cheat on his wife, he'll cheat on you." But I think she discovered on her own that all the frauds required to keep their adultery going made it difficult for her to keep loving Phillip Alton Whyte, and made her feel rotten about herself. And then it threatened to make her son rotten, too.

"Hello, Mr. Washington!" my mother greeted the man with the respiration machine. "I don't believe that you've met my son."

"No, ma'am. Sure haven't."

We shook hands. Mr. Washington had a soft, sure grip, and a deep, rolling river of a speaking voice. He had a bow tie and a gleaming smile. My mother began to tell me about where he went to church.

"He's a soloist in the choir. Can't you just tell from how he says hello what a gorgeous voice he has?" I could. "Mr. Washington, my son uses his voice, too."

"But it's not nearly as nice as yours," I told him.

"I'll have this hooked up and ready in a moment," said Mr. Washington. It sounded like he was introducing an aria. "Your mom. We've been having some great conversations. You two go on visiting."

I took my mother's hand again, and she returned to her low voice.

"I realized I had to do something when I realized that we couldn't keep hiding things from you," she said. "I realized that I was showing you all the wrong things about love."

Mr. Washington made deft, quick movements over his machine. He popped the cellophane bag over an oxygen mask.

"Do you think you'll see Phillip again? Whenever?"

Whenever had become our way to refer to whatever eternity would soon follow. My mother scrunched up her eyes and chin and made a naughty-little-girl face just before Mr. Washington's skilled and silken hands pulled the plastic breathing mask over her smile.

"Oh. Sure. We'll have a drink. And I'll send him on his way. I'm sure he hasn't lost his roving eye. You know, dear, he always wanted to meet Liz Taylor."

And yes, wish my family was here. But want our daughters just to remember the Grandmere who lavished them w/ smiles.

12

Nights are the hardest. But that's why I'm here. I wish I could lift my mother's pain & fears from her bones into mine.

After Mr. Washington had deflated the bag and unplugged his machinery from my mother, she rubbed a fresh tissue over her nose. It looked as red as the nose of a child who has been crying through his first fever.

"All that," she said, "just to breathe. That used to be as easy as breathing."

"Oooh, that's a good line," I told her.

"I've run out of people to tell good lines to," she said. "I miss my friends."

"I miss your friends, too," I told her.

My mother rejiggered her oxygen tubes and sighed.

"I hated seeing so many people I loved grow old and get sick," she said. "See them lose their grip. Or just disappear into one of those storage cabinets." I suppose she meant housing blocks for senior citizens. "Or a basement in the suburbs." I suppose she meant a spare room in the house of a grown son or daughter.

She looked up.

"What was it Ralph said? 'I don't need to look in a mirror anymore. I see enough familiar faces in the obituaries.'"

I stood up to take my mother's hand.

"You have friends for years, then lose them in bunches. Remember Biruta?"

I nodded.

"She went inch by inch, to cancer. That beautiful woman," she said, closing her eyes. "Or Eleanor. Goes to the drugstore one day, and something inside her head explodes. Melba and Abba . . ." She left space for me to recall a few more.

"You lose them, or just lose touch. I loved them," she said. "Darlene, Peggy. So many. They loved us."

For years my mother's constant running mate and gal pal was the woman we called Auntie Chris. She'd come to Chicago from a Greek family in Iowa (birth name: Chrisoula), and indeed possessed the kind of silhouette art teachers and gentlemen used to call "classical." Her Aphrodite form helped her find work as a hostess and dancer in clubs along Rush Street when she first hit town, which is where she met my mother (and, she said, bundles of big-toothed, tousle-haired Kennedy boys, sitting with Chicago mobsters).

Chris was hardheaded and droll. She was an outspoken Iowa Republican who was suspicious of what she saw as the local blarney, guff, and moonshine, and thought that my mother, whom she loved, could be sweetly naïve about men, business, and Democrats.

Chris eventually went to work in the personnel department of an auto company, and did very well. She saw this as the consequence of common sense, not rising feminism.

"Burn their bras!" she'd exclaim, standing tall with Iowa *zaftig*. "Why would these gals want to burn their bras? My *bra* is my best friend!"

Chris was with us in front of the television when we watched Jacqueline Kennedy's slow, noble walk behind the casket of her murdered husband.

"I hate to say it," Chris announced. "But Jackie's better off without him. I still see his girlfriend around here. Beautiful gal. Looks like Liz Taylor. She's one of Momo Giancana's gals, too. I'm sorry for Jackie, but believe me, she's better off without—" and my mother, who loved Chris and cherished her independent thinking, cut her short.

"Oh, Chris, not now, please. Not that Republican mumbo-jumbo." (All mumbo-jumbo we later learned turned out to be more or less true.)

There was Melba, a media buyer for whom my mother worked as a secretary at an ad agency on Michigan Avenue.

"The *creatives* drink expense-account martinis for lunch and nap in their offices," Melba said, years before *Mad Men*. "We actually earn a little money for the company."

Melba gleamed. She was silvery, saucy, and the wit in my mother's circle whom all waited to hear. One night, someone in the group came back from a drugstore with one of the first dental machines that spurts water through your gums. You filled a small tank, held up a wand, pressed a button, and a hard burst of water (*spume*, I dare say, is the right word) spurted from the nozzle.

My mother and her friends filled the tank over and over. They giggled as it gushed and dripped, gushed and dripped. They aimed the spurts at each other, like kids at a squirt gun fight, tittering, "Oooh, it likes you," and, "Oooh, it doesn't last very long."

The laughter wound down after we'd filled the tank half a

dozen times and saw numerous . . . emissions. I think a couple of the women lit cigarettes. Melba waited for the quiet to ask, "And could you also use that on your teeth?"

I had no idea what she meant; I knew Melba was hilarious.

There was Auntie Abba, who was blond, tall, slim, and walked like a samba, to recall a phrase of the time, as she balanced a Chicago phone book on her head (which she did many times for me and my friends).

Auntie Abba may have been the first person I knew who spoke with a British accent. She was about as British as Dolly Parton. Abba was from Baton Rouge, and worked for her posh enunciation as assiduously as actors from the Royal Shakespeare Company now learn bayou accents to play Americans.

"I won't have people up here ask me just about corn likker and skinning alligators," she said, which was a pretty faithful approximation of some of the ideas Chicagoans could have about Southerners.

Auntie Abba trained Playboy Bunnies for clubs around the country. She taught the Playboy way to smile, say hello, and deliver drinks with the Bunny Dip, the maneuver by which they could put a Blue Hawaiian in front of a customer without revealing cleavage.

Chicago's Playboy Club was considered, aside from the political critiques that had begun, a good place to work. They paid well, promoted from within (Auntie Abba had been a Bunny at the Miami and St. Louis clubs), and sent the late-night serving crew home in cabs. Moreover, as Abba put it, "Mr. Hefner will brook no shit from big-spending arseholes," meaning that a patron who tried to put his palm on a Bunny's bum or hector her with a lewd remark would be given the heave-ho onto Walton Street, no matter who he was or how much money he had spilled.

"And you should see some of the people I've seen thrown out," she'd tell us, although careful to uphold the company's vow of confidentiality. "Oscar winners. Senators. Mobsters. Mr. Hefner insists on courtesy to all."

Abba disdained (and when Abba dripped disdain, it was a powerful, toxic stream) the criticism Gloria Steinem had made of Playboy's bunny costumes as being painful and demeaning.

"Uniforms," Abba corrected all. "*Uniforms.* And they wear some pretty painful and ridiculous costumes at the Metropolitan Opera, too."

Over the years, I think I've quoted Auntie Abba more times than any presidential inaugural address I've covered. And I think she and Gloria Steinem would have liked each other.

Auntie Geri was a manicurist. She had wide blue eyes, short red hair, and ivory skin. Geri worked some of the swankier hair salons on the Near North Side, and would tell her friends, "I had the nicest client today. A Mr. Roselli. He's in the movie business."

I remember Auntie Chris taking a long, slow breath on a cigarette.

"Handsome Johnny?"

"He was pretty handsome, yes. A little old, maybe."

(Johnny Roselli, aka "Handsome Johnny," was found in an oil drum at the bottom of Biscayne Bay about a dozen years later. He was wanted by fellow members of the Chicago mob for skimming money; by the U.S. Congress, who wanted him to testify about being hired by the Kennedy brothers to whack Fidel Castro; and by conspiracy buffs, who wanted him to comment on the hearsay that he'd been involved in a hit on President Kennedy.)

Women as well as men often dismissed Auntie Geri on nothing more than her faun-like looks. She thought cigarettes stank, so she chewed gum—which was wiser and healthier, but did not make Geri look much like, say, Simone de Beauvoir.

Yet Geri read widely and could be sharp in her judgments. She'd inherit the folded copies of the *New York Times* and *Wall Street Journal* her clients left behind, many of the small headlines bleary with water drops. Auntie Geri would blot the newspapers, read them through the day, and often bring them to me, marked with red arrows and circles.

"See the story on Indonesia—just terrible killings going on there. And they keep writing about this play about a very sick Frenchman, but honestly, he doesn't sound worth a whole play to me."

(Years later, I saw a production of Peter Weiss's *Marat/Sade* and was impressed. But I think Auntie Geri had a point.)

And there was Auntie Marion, a former lounge singer who performed up and down Rush Street before marrying Charlie Grimm, the old Chicago Cubs first baseman and manager (though they had met when Jolly Cholly, as he had been known, played the banjo at the Club Alabam).

Marion had sung with Bing Crosby in a musical short. She had played the 500 Club with Nat King Cole. She was a featured extra in *The Babe Ruth Story*, a movie I have seen a dozen times without quite being sure if the caramel-haired beauty you can see in black and white cheering the Bambino is Auntie Marion.

Marion believed that cigarettes "sweetened" a voice, and did a lot of sweetening. For years she carried a fluffy little white pompom of a poodle named Sugar in her purse. She wouldn't get home until after the last set and a last drink, at two or three in the morning. That was not a good time to walk a dog who couldn't bite through a jelly donut. So Marion spread the *Tribune* over the kitchen floor of her studio apartment (a room she otherwise might see only to get fresh ice cubes for scotch), where Sugar could drop her "sweet little fudgie-sicles."

Little Sugar would squat and quiver over the unfurled front page. Auntie Chris would shout, "Aim for Mayor Daley! Aim for Mayor Daley!"

"Do you remember when we had to spring Chris and Marion from jail?" my mother asked from her hospital bed.

"Highlight of my childhood," I told her.

The telephone rang one night, in the days when it jangled: Auntie Chris said that she and Marion were in prison. Well, they were being booked at the Chicago Avenue police station at any rate, and needed help.

Auntie Chris told my mother in a tumble that they'd gone out for a hamburger on Wells Street, Marion driving. They saw the blue light in the rearview mirror, and heard the growl of a siren, so they pulled over. A young policeman came to the driver's side to say they'd missed a stop sign. When Marion replied something like, "Well, I'm *sooo sorry,* dear," the policeman sniffed more than a whiff of beer. When he asked to see her license, she patted her pockets, flipped open her purse, and announced, "Imagine that. Guess I forgot."

The police officer suggested Auntie Chris take over the wheel to drive home. But when he asked to see her license—which she'd just remembered that she'd left in her purse in front of her door— she'd replied, "Is that what things are coming to in this town under Dick Daley? You need a license to run out for a hamburger?"

I remember the tone of wonder and worry in my mother's voice when she heard this account as she said softly, "Oh, Chris . . ."

What my mother said now was, "They were lucky the police didn't drag them to Devil's Island."

That night we had pulled on clothes, as if we'd heard a fire bell. We looked for bail money, in the days before automated teller machines, and my mother plucked a stack of twenties she'd tucked under tissue paper in her lingerie drawer. We snagged a cab on North State Parkway, and I got to tell the driver, "Chicago Avenue police station, please. And step on it!"

The station house was blindingly bright inside, and crackled and squawked with police radios. A pretty mother with her son in tow drew stares.

"Good morning, Captain," my mother told the desk sergeant, as if he were the captain of a cruise ship. "We'd like to see a couple of your guests. . . ."

(My mother was the daughter of a Chicago police sergeant, and knew the difference between a sergeant's stripes and a captain's bars. But because she was a policeman's daughter, she also knew to flatter an officer with the title of a higher rank.)

The desk sergeant didn't need to consult his blotter. A blue circle of officers surrounded aunties Chris and Marion, who were, somewhat to my disappointment, unshackled. Marion roosted on the edge of a desk.

" 'Someday he'll come along,' " she sang in a smoky, dusky voice. " 'And he'll be big and strong, the man I love . . .' " An inspired choice for a station house.

There was no arrest, no bail, just the mildest reminder from the police to stop at stop signs and carry your license when operating a motor vehicle. A kitten-haired young patrolman told Marion, "Sure, I'm a cop, but really, I want to be a singer."

She took his hand and brushed it with her lips.

"Follow your dream, darling," she told him.

I sat on my mother's lap in the cab riding back north, Chris and Marion cackling beside us.

"The second sergeant we saw was handsome."

"Married for sure."

"You checked his hand?"

"Don't you?"

"The lieutenant was a better dresser."

"Officers get better uniforms. But believe me," said Auntie Chris, "they all wind up wearing those funny little golf shirts and saggy slacks."

My mother leaned behind my ear to tell me, "I don't want you to think that jail is always this much fun."

What I remember of that group of women from my boyhood is: lingering, impromptu evenings with lots of snorts and laughs, olives and cheddar cheese on rye crackers, the stroke of matches, the tinkle of ice, compact makeup mirrors folded with a snap, high heels under the coffee table, crinkled cocktail napkins with lipstick smudges, earrings pulled out and resting on a coaster, Tony Bennett on the turntable, an occasional crying jag, and the orange glow of cigarettes, candles, and streetlights just below the windows. I don't remember (or more likely didn't recognize) profound conversations. But I knew that the buzz of laughs and gossip was a fizz that refilled my mother and her friends.

Most of the women in her circle had been married at least once; a couple would be again. My mother thought one or two might have preferred women, but in those times, finding the right man was believed to be therapy for that. Single, working women have children on their own today; my mother didn't think most of her friends would have wanted that. Instead, these tough, funny, and resilient women turned their care and tenderness on the child in front of them.

"They loved you so," my mother said now.

"I loved them. I was blessed. Do you remember the year I was an astronaut for Halloween? All those helping hands."

"All that silver spray paint," my mother recalled. "Do you remember Gordon?"

"Sort of."

"Handsome guy. Ad exec with . . ." She recalled the three names of the firm (three initials now).

"Dimples."

"And slick hair. We had dinner once or twice. He always wanted to have lunch just with you. He made me uncomfortable. He kept saying, 'Don't you worry about your son spending all that time with gals and swishes? How is he going to learn how to be a real man?'"

"He wasn't a classy guy," I told my mother. "I remember that now."

My mother didn't worry, much less care, that I might be gay, or no good at baseball (in fact, I was already perceptibly interested in girls, as well as musicals, and pretty good at baseball and track). She did worry that my father—funny, sweet, but irresponsible and weak against drink—would not give me the image of the kind of man even he would want me to grow up to be.

But my mother's friends (and my father, for that matter) passed on to me a phrase for the kind of man they admired: *a classy guy*.

The accolade had nothing to do with money, business, or breeding. Ernie Banks and my school principal, Mort Reisman, were classy guys, and so were Adlai Stevenson, Nat King Cole, Sir Noël Coward, and the man who drove the #36 bus down State Street.

A classy guy had manners. He said please and thank you, Mr.

and Miss, and held open doors. Classy guys picked up checks. They left good tips. They dressed with respect. They kept their word. They sent flowers. They apologized personally. They tried to be kind and courteous, even if they sometimes had to be firm, and their best jokes were about themselves.

My mother's friends had learned all this by knowing a few classy guys, and many who weren't. Mistakes, good times, lonely nights, and hard-won laughs had taught them what counted in a man's character. They passed what they learned on to me in dozens of stories. They gave me something to steer toward.

My mother's circle of friends also gave me a glimpse of good friendship. Friends were the people you called at 3 A.M. to get you out of jail, but they were also the people who were with you at 9 P.M. on a slow Saturday night. Friends shared crises and they shared what was often the trickier test of tedium. My mother's humor and strength sometimes made it hard to see how much of her life had been busted. But her friendships with such rugged, chic, and appealing women gave her other lives to care about and gave hers purpose, shape, and laughter.

The tick of years—marriages, moves, and illness—scattered my mother's circle. But their memories kept a hold on each other and, I grew to appreciate, gave them a stake in me.

"People move," my mother told me now. "They die. They get tired and just want to crawl into a hole. It's life, and it's a shame. But now and then, I'd hear from one of the gals. And every time they'd ask, 'How's our boy?' They'd say, 'I guess our boy turned out okay.'"

Thanks for all good wishes. Mother says, "We can get through this, baby. The hardest part we'll be for you when it's over"

13

**I tell her, "You've given me strength to carry it."
She's reciting White Cliffs of Dover now, becoming
14 before my eyes.**

My mother would have a respiration treatment and seem to
breathe a little more easily, then she'd talk to me, which would
seem to talk the air out of the lung and a half that she had. She
would shut her eyes and try to rest her mind, and then begin to
gasp.

I put my hands on her shoulders. She put her head against
mine, found a breath, and then dropped back to her pillow.

"I'm fine," she'd say. "Really. Now."

"Try to breathe," I'd advise uselessly.

"It's like . . . I swallowed a bottle of turpentine. It stings down
there. So much," she said.

My mother took a breath, the way you might before ducking your
head underwater, then began to recite:

"I have loved England, dearly and deeply,
Since that first morning, shining and pure,
The white cliffs of Dover I saw rising steeply . . ."

I had grown up hearing my mother—my *Irish* mother—recite verses of Alice Duer Miller's poem. I knew she had learned it to audition for Chicago's Goodman School of Drama shortly after she'd turned nineteen, and had spent the season in summer stock in Denver. My mother painted scenery, spoke a few lines onstage as various maids and miladys, and learned (she had pictures) how to ride a horse.

It was her first summer out of high school—*Catholic* high school—and she used to laugh, recalling how her mother had arrived for a visit, saw so many visibly handsome and excited young people vying for attention and staying up late in the same bunkhouse to drink and dance to Nat King Cole, that she asked her daughter, "So, is everybody sleeping with everybody around here?"

My mother said she just laughed and replied, "It's the theatah, mother dear."

(Years later she told me, "Mother had nothing to worry about. Only a couple of guys were straight.")

I remember seeing a photo of the group of young people who worked at the Elitch Garden Theater that summer, hoisting each other on their shoulders and cavorting onstage in boas and hats. My mother pointed to a notably cool, coifed blonde.

"Grace Kelly," she said. The future Most Serene Highness was beautiful. But if you saw my mother and Princess Grace in the same photo, you'd think they both deserved a small kingdom.

My mother returned to Chicago and auditioned for the Goodman with *White Cliffs*. Alice Duer Miller's poem is a novel in verse that tells the story of a young American woman who comes to London and falls for a noble young Englishman who goes on to die in World War I. She stays because she has really fallen in love with England. As the story ends, she wonders if she will lose the son she had with her late husband to the Second World War, now raging overhead and just across the Channel from those white cliffs. The poem became fantastically popular when it was published in 1940. Britain was imperial and imperiled, and it seemed to solidify the case in an isolationist-minded United States that England's survival was essential. The same roots nourished us:

> *The tree of Liberty grew and changed and spread,*
> *But the seed was English*

My mother thought it was a wonderful audition piece. She could fall in love, lose her love, give birth, struggle with grief, and grow from a love-struck young girl into a mature mother in half an hour.

I also think the poem spoke of her feeling for England. My mother was proud to be Irish, and for that matter, Belfast Catholic Irish. But she admired British liberties, wit, literature, and style. She loved Shakespeare, tattersall, Churchill, Dame Judi, and tweeds, Colin Firth, bold stripes, music hall, and Monty Python.

The Irish Republicans of my mother's youth seemed to be mostly at war with each other. My mother was not political. But she considered Britain the cultural capital of the civilized world, an empire that gave its colonies, from America to Ireland to India, the means and inspiration to break free. My mother didn't long to be British. She thought that we, Americans and Irish, kind of already were, or as the poem put it:

And were they not English, our forefathers, never more

. . . . .

. . . English than when they dared to be
Rebels against her . . .

My mother spoke with a mild brogue as a child. I never heard it (or rather, I heard it just a few times, when she had a few sips more than a second glass of wine). Her mother had a slight brogue; her father said, "Dere's dese guys dat I know. . . ." But my mother always *pro-noun-ced ev-ry con-so-nant and vow-el cor-rect-ly,* which could make the man from whom she ordered a corned beef sandwich at Eli's Stage Deli feel like he worked at the Ritz.

"I didn't try to lose my brogue," she told me a few years ago. "I just outgrew it. I wasn't ashamed. I was proud of being Irish. But I didn't want to be *typecast* Irish. In *life*. Brogues weren't cute then. They were a ball and chain. Gals who spoke with brogues only played scullery maids. Gals who spoke with brogues applied for jobs at the Drake Hotel and got hired as maids or elevator operators. Not the front desk."

My mother auditioned for, but did not get into, the Goodman School of Drama. Years later, she'd see Bella Itkin, the eminent acting teacher with whom she had interviewed, at various plays around town.

"You should have stayed with it, Patricia."

"Oh, really, Dr. Itkin . . . ," she'd reply, and laugh away the small bouquet.

I met Dr. Itkin a few times and once took her aside at a theater event.

"I really do remember your mother's audition," she said. "She was darling. But she didn't keep trying."

"She got married. She had me. That was *really* trying. She had a daughter who died, then her mother, a tough marriage . . ."

"She shouldn't have taken the first no she got," said Dr. Itkin. "She was a darling."

I stretched this a little, later that night, with my mother.

"Dr. Itkin thinks you could have been another Redgrave."

"Oh, fiddlesticks. Even if," she said. "All the people she taught, and how many famous names do we keep hearing?"

"Joe Mantegna. Linda Hunt. Uh, uh . . ."

"Exactly. I would have been one of those uhs . . ."

Years fell away as my mother recited her audition piece. I was glad that our daughters knew her as a doting, indulgent grandmother who laid feasts in front of them and listened to their tea party conversations with dolls. I told them stories about the young mother I had known growing up, who had taken me on buses and cable cars to pretty, empty little city parks when I was a sickly little boy, where she had rolled balls to me and swung me onto her shoulders with a shower of giggles. I told our daughters some of the same stories she had told me at night, looking out our window over the streetlights, settling on a star, and saying, "Sleep peacefully, baby. That big bright star is looking over you."

But I sometimes regretted that they knew her only as a grandmother.

"Making cinnamon toast for you wasn't always the highlight of Grand-mère's day, you know," I sometimes told them. "Your grandmother used to travel in some pretty fast company. She was the funniest woman in Chicago. She was the Jon James Hairspray Girl. She saw Frank, Dino, and Sammy."

I saw my mother's age, pain, and exhaustion as I sat with her in her room, her thinning hair and trembling hands. But as she recalled and recited the verses she had learned when she was young and driven by so many dreams, I began to glimpse a funny, flirty, and dishy nineteen-year-old, too, a cop's daughter who tried to speak posh for the stage.

> *"I had no thought then of husband or lover,*
> *I was a traveller, the guest of a week;*
> *Yet when they pointed 'the white cliffs of Dover,'*
> *Startled I found there were tears on my cheek. . . ."*

I could see my mother go from girl to grandmother, like a character from a historical drama. The stage performed its old role to help us see and feel, laugh and cry, and my mother, who had never quite made it onstage, gave me the performance of a lifetime.

> *"I am American bred,*
> *I have seen much to hate here—much to forgive,*
> *But in a world where England is finished and dead,*
> *I do not wish to live."*

No real sleep tonight. But songs poems memories laughs. My mother: "Thank you God for giving us this night & each other"

That will be my life's slogan from now on.

14

My mother: "Believe me, those great death bed speeches are written ahead of time."

No one had told my mother that she would soon die. But she had once been the mother of a teenager, after all, and saw how the young residents who came to her bed now spoke in a rushed, tense jumble of jargon and would not meet her eyes. "They blather something and back out," she said, "like they left the motor running."

Most of all, my mother could feel that her lungs were beginning to wear out, like a set of bald tires. She fought for breath, but her lungs couldn't hold it. A doctor told me months later that when you're sick like my mother was, you feel that you're in a bed in a downtown hospital surrounded by nurses and trussed up in wires and tubes that are threaded into the most sensitive machines, but you're drowning. Everyone sees it, and no one can help you. As your lungs begin to deflate, it feels as if a heavy band is being tightened inside your chest, and the more you gasp, the less you breathe. You begin to tell yourself, more in certainty than panic: This must be how I'm going to die.

I squeezed her hand and my mother squeezed her eyes shut.

She said, "Help me, Mother . . ."

She kept her eyes closed and I crept onto her bed.

"Can you see your mother?" I asked after a while, and a long moment went by.

"Maybe," said my mother. "Maybe."

"I can," I told her, and in that moment, I could. "I see Granny. I see Frances. Her dazzling silver hair. Her gorgeous smile. Those brown-green eyes. She's smiling."

"Is she stretching her hand?"

"Yes."

"Yes."

We were mother and son, looking up into the stars again, in cahoots to see the same unicorn.

I suggested, "Why don't we both reach out for her hand?"

"You've got to stay here."

"I'll see you through the door. I'll hold on to you," I said, and slid next to my mother on the top of her bed and put an arm around her shoulders.

"You taught me—a gentleman always sees a lady to the door."

My mother shuddered to close her eyes tighter. I felt the squeeze in her neck and saw water trickle from her eyes as she tried to will herself through the door we had connived to see, where her mother offered her hand. I said to whoever hears such messages, "We're ready. *Now*. Please. We're ready. *Now*."

But after another long moment, my mother opened her eyes and let her head sink back into a pillow.

"Oh hell," she said. "My mother never helped me anyway."

My memories of my grandmother, Frances Julia Sullivan, my mother's mother, come wrapped in sugar and smoke. I remember her pink hands presenting me with sugar-sprinkled cookies and cocoa with whipped cream peaks, her pillowy red lips blowing smoky kisses, and her fabulous platinum hair swishing over her bare pink shoulders as she leaned down to kiss the top of my head.

"Love ya madly," she'd always say.

And I remember, or anyhow, I think I do, her pink toes peeking out below the piano where we found her Thanksgiving morning when I was about four, even as my father put an arm over my eyes and my mother gasped and sprang forward and he rammed my head into his shoulder, as if there was a bomb going off. I guess there was.

Frances was stunning. That was the word you always heard. The dark eyes, glowing with flecks of green, her hair ablaze like polished silver, her brash and brassy laugh.

I've heard various stories as to how she first came to the United States from Ireland, or to Chicago from Quebec, that I haven't been able to resolve. But they seem to agree that the man she would marry, Francis Joseph Lyons, had known her since their childhoods, growing up in the immigrant Irish precincts of Oak Park and Chicago's Southwest Side.

(I inherited the high Lyons hairline—and Francis's diabetes— and the platinum Sullivan hair, albeit to less sensational effect.)

Francis became a Chicago police sergeant. He was handsome, moody, meticulous (I still recall the precision with which he would slice an apple), and a little lackluster. He liked fishing, "The Rose of Tralee," boiled cabbage and potatoes; he would let a beer warm up a little before taking the first sip.

Frances was glamorous, humorous, spontaneous, and sometimes a little scattered. She loved nightspots, "Stompin' at the Savoy," Shrimp De Jonghe, and Gibson martinis, which she'd down in a flash.

Some in my mother's Irish family were appalled when she brought home a "Hee-brew" (as my grandfather drew out the word) comedian. But Frances would meet my father at the door when we came to their apartment.

"Hello, Big Ern, love ya madly," she'd say, shaking a shiny silver cocktail shaker, dappled with cool beads, as if to dazzle a child.

"Baby wants his bottle," he'd reply, and they'd down the pitcher together, refill, shake, rattle, roll, and knock back another.

Frances became the hostess of the Cape Cod Room in the Drake Hotel, in the days when nearly fresh seafood from ocean waters, cloaked in cream, was an exotic catch in the Midwest. She got jobs at the Drake, too, for a whole raft of Lyonses and Sullivans. They served, shook sheets and tablecloths, chopped onions and bussed tables. In the Cape Cod Room, beefy Chicago bankers or steel execs would ask my grandmother, "Frances, honey, send a *mick* over to clear our table, won't you, babe?" The young man working for tips whom my grandmother would send over was often one of her nephews.

When Francis shook off another round, people would think he had a stingy spirit. When Frances ordered another round all around, it was taken as a token of her vivacity. I came to cast them in my mind: Francis dutiful but dull, Frances the sheer bubbling delight; two abiding Catholics trapped in a spiritless marriage that they kept afloat, if not alive, by leading separate lives.

My mother laughed to recall a night at Fritzel's Restaurant on State Street. While Sergeant Francis worked the overnight shift to protect the city, my mother and father took Frances to a supper club.

A handsome, mature man came to the bar to fetch drinks for

his table, including his wife, and made it a point to stand with my father.

"Who's your wife's friend?" he asked.

"Her mother. My *mother-in-law,* Frances," my father emphasized.

"Oh my God."

"Yes."

"Oh my God."

"I know."

"I've never asked a question like this before," the man told my father, "but does your mother-in-law fool around?"

Granny took me on lunch dates. My mother would suds, scrub, and polish me until rosy, part and pat down my hair, and pull my little pink legs through tickly wool pants until I looked like a little gentleman (in particular the *Life* magazine pictures she'd once seen of little Prince Charlie out for a stroll). We'd sit with Granny's friends in a banquette at the Drake or the Palmer House, where I'd have a hot fudge sundae, a sidecar of extra fudge alongside, and when we returned to our apartment my mother would wring out a washcloth to swab little gobs of crusted fudge from my face.

"Did you have a good time with Granny, baby?"

"Oh yes. We had lunch with Mildred." Or Gladys, Clara, Lillian, or Dorothy.

One night my father took Frances and Francis to dinner with our family. Waiters plopped a phone book, cloaked in a napkin, for me to sit on the plump cream-colored cushions of a booth in the Pump Room. They brought out flaming things on skewers. My father told jokes and spun out stories that made Frances giggle, while Francis, who never quite knew when the punch line had landed, would ask, "What? What did you say? Why is that funny?"

An elegant couple walked by on the way to their table, and I waved at the handsome greyhound of a husband.

"Gladys! Gladys!"

The husband struggled to appear puzzled. It may have been the first time I'd seen an older man blush.

"Gladys! Gladys! Remember me?"

I kept calling the name as he tried to walk away, so the man called Gladys came back to our table.

"What a darling little boy," he said, without much conviction. "I guess I must remind him of someone."

"Gladys! Gladys!" I began to cry. "Don't you remember me?"

The man looked at my mother, looked at my father, and gave a feeble little wag of his fingers to me.

"Of course my name isn't Gladys," he added. "I've never met your most charming little boy," and awarded me another little flutter of his fingers.

My mother could feel her mother shift in her seat alongside her, and turned to see that Frances had hoisted a huge, velvet-clad menu in front of her face.

"Gladys! Gladys! Gladys!"

Tears rolled down my face as I cried, "Gladys! Gladys!" while the man quickly rejoined his wife (who might have been as wise to her husband as my mother was to her mother), and Frances rested her forehead behind the wine list. She was laughing.

"Gladys!" I called, and cried as the man picked up his pace, and my mother ducked her head behind her mother's velvet barricade.

"Gladys? Mildred? Dorothy?"

Most of this account, of course, is from my mother's vivid

memories of that night, and her practiced retelling. But I am pretty sure I can recall the muted tone of a scold in my mother's voice—it was the one that, every now and then, she used on me—as she turned to Frances and told her, "Mother, *really* . . ."

"Men were always drawn to my mother," my mother would tell me years later. "And when she went to work at the Drake, they could call her to make reservations."

One Thanksgiving, we took a cab out to the West Side apartment that Frances and Francis shared between night shifts and separations. My mother's arms were full with a pumpkin chiffon pie and kitchen implements, spilling from a brown bag, and my father's arms were filled with me. Sergeant Francis was at the station house, and would be home in the middle of the afternoon to carve the turkey. Frances had said she would be knee-deep in frozen cranberries, green beans, and Cheez Whiz, so my mother should use her key.

We trooped up three flights of stairs. The whiff of roasting turkey hung in the halls. The sound of strings from a classical music station wafted from under an apartment door. My mother turned the key. My father set me down. My mother called out, "We're here, Mother!" and I began to scamper into the kitchen for hugs, kisses, and cocoa when my mother gasped and I saw Granny in the living room, napping with her eyes open under the upright piano.

There were two empty brown bottles nearby: one of a morning's worth of scotch, the other of a month's supply of sleeping pills.

I was sixteen, and my father had died, before my mother felt I was old enough for her to tell me, without genteelisms, that my grandmother had committed suicide. As years went by, when she thought I had seen a little more in life, she filled in the details. But she worried because she'd learned that suicide is a family contagion. It passes between generations. It plants a time bomb in your family tree. It opens a door in your mind in your darkest moments, so you think you glimpse some sweet relief on the other side, but it leaves just guilt, doubt, and desolation for those you love and leave behind, and it doesn't make them—make anyone—love you.

My mother loved her mother, but more: she was also her closest pal, her confidante, the person who told her dirty jokes, shopped for shoes with her, and shared crazy gossip.

But now, in the ICU, my mother opened her eyes wide and told me, "My mother took the next few years of my life away from me. I didn't go to bed a single night without thinking, 'What if I had gotten there five minutes earlier? What if she didn't really mean to? What did we miss? Why didn't she tell me?' You can't be happy like that."

I rolled over onto an elbow. It reminded me of the way my mother would prop herself next to my pillow to listen to my stories at night.

"Frances didn't leave a note?" I asked, and my mother shook her head.

"Nothing. Nothing on the piano, in the kitchen, or on her pillow. For a long time, I thought that meant that she didn't really mean it. I thought she knew we'd be there to save her and laugh about it all. She had dinner waiting. She'd even put out the silver."

"Who knows what she was thinking? She was sad and desperate."

"And why didn't I know that?" my mother asked. "That's what

you ask yourself. Over and over. 'Why didn't she tell me any-thing?' I thought she told me everything.

"I figured, 'Maybe she sent me a letter.' I checked the mail for weeks. Really, for *years*. You'd see some story about someone who mailed something during the war, and it fell behind a wall, or got misrouted to Missouri, and didn't get delivered for twenty years. So I'd get the mail even years later, and see some envelope with half-familiar handwriting and think . . ."

My mother closed her eyes again. I sat up beside her.

"Whatever she did—or why—it wasn't your fault."

"I could have tried to stop some of her drinking. I just served her one after another."

"She was your mother."

"Yes. And she left me all alone. With a little boy and a hus-band drinking himself to death."

"She loved you. She must have been desperate."

"She was drunk—all the time. I don't know why they call booze liquid courage," said my mother as she closed her eyes again. "It should be called liquid stupidity."

A few days after Frances's death, an urbane, handsome man who was a union leader and had often dined at the Drake took his life near my grandmother's grave site. The newspapers hinted at financial problems and investigations. But his widow called my mother to say our family was not welcome at her husband's funeral.

A month later, my grandfather Francis told my mother he was getting married. To a woman named Rosemary, a typist at the station house, who had told him (actually, her three burly broth-ers had so informed him) that she was pregnant (she was not).

My mother recalled relating all this to my father as they

dangled in adjoining swings in the backyard of our apartment building, while I shouted, "Push me! Higher!"

"My God," my mother remembered my father saying. "Married. And Frances isn't even cold in her grave."

It astonishes me now to see how little, until this point, my grandfather enters these recollections. He often worked double shifts when my mother was growing up, but was home most days by the time I was a toddler, and would spend hours watching me in my crib and playing with me. He often brought me to his station house, where I was booked and fingerprinted, and posed for smiling mug shots.

My grandfather had not been happy to see my mother marry my father. She was too young; they had just met; he was too Jewish. Francis could utter astonishingly twisted things about Jews (and Poles, blacks, Hispanics, Lithuanians, Asians, Serbians, Bosnians, Estonians, Italians, Sicilians, homosexuals, Protestants, and, I'm quite sure, Martians, if they'd ever landed on the South Side). But my grandfather's paternal suspicion that my mother could have found a better husband than my father was not misguided, even though I am blessed to be their son.

My grandmother's death, and my grandfather's whirlwind remarriage, reinforced the idea that he hadn't deserved the dazzling Frances, and that his sulking and stinginess had driven her under the piano bench.

My mother and her father grew even farther apart after her mother's suicide. For most of my life we blamed this on Rosemary. She didn't like Jews. She thought they (which is to say *we*) were uncouth, scheming, and slippery. She made a sloppy, drunken phone call one night to say she was sorry we weren't closer, but she *woooved* her vewwy pwetty daughter and her wittle gwandshon, and even her Hee-bwew shon-in-law (drunken emphasis mine). My father told her (I believe this is word for word), "I'd believe you more if you got off your fat keister and saw your grandson now and then." Rosemary answered that she had tried not to believe all the terrible things people said about Jews, but now she knew they were true, and (I am sure this is word for word), "I hope everything that happens to you from now on is bad."

Which, my mother often noted thereafter, it pretty much was. My father drank himself out of jobs, then into his grave. My mother had to leave him, start over, and support us, all without the aid and comfort of her father.

But now I think of how hard it must have been for my grandfather to look at his daughter and not be reminded of all the secrets that, out of loyalty to her mother, she had kept from him. The colluding looks and laughs my mother and Frances traded behind the wine list in that booth must have hurt him beyond Gladys, Mildred, and Dorothy.

Francis died just a year after my father. I was seventeen and my hair brushed my shoulders, at a time when Chicago police were still renowned for beating people with hair as long as mine with billy clubs. But a lot of long-haired people (and African-American police officers, and African-American and Hispanic families, and unshaven street people) came to his funeral to salute Sergeant Francis Joseph Lyons. He was apparently the kind of cop who slipped quarters to panhandlers and sandwiches to hungry street people. His fellow officers who were black and had heard him utter epithets shrugged them off. "Police stations are rough places. That's how we all talk." I'm sure a lot of people with better social and political ideas haven't done as much for as many as my grandfather did.

Ralph Newman was convicted almost two decades after Frances took her life. It was also November. Holiday lights already

blinked along State Street. As we crowded into the elevator after the jury returned, the smooth music piped in went, "Outside
the snow is falling and friends are calling, 'Yoo-hoo!'" Ralph
would be sentenced in early December and a parole officer would
interview each member of the family. My mother and I ended
Thanksgiving night over a bottle of wine.

"Suicide runs in families," she said.

"I know."

"Look at the Hemingways. I told Merle"—Ralph's parole
officer—"about my mother."

"She has to know."

"The judge might go easy on Ralph if he thought I'd . . . do
something."

I sat up to put down my glass as my mother went on.

"And then I thought: I could take something, you know. Then
call you."

"What if my phone was out?" I asked her. "What if the subway got stuck?"

"You wouldn't take a cab?"

My mother made a sour little face.

"Thanks a lot, son of mine," she said, but lightly. We cackled
the thought away.

But now, in the ICU, my mother closed her eyes as if to put herself back in that night, the wine bottle between us.

"That must have scared you. I'm sorry."

"Well, I scared you a few times, too."

(I wasn't thinking of the wars I covered, so much as my ado-
lescence.)

"Do you know what sheet music was on the piano when my

mother died there?" she asked. "'We'll Meet Again.'" My mother began to sing and I joined her.

"*'Don't know how, don't know when, but I know we'll meet again . . . dh-dah-dah-dah . . .'*"

She opened her eyes and raised her head.

"Do you think that meant something?"

"I don't know," I told her. "But I think it's true."

"All the running around my mother did," she said. "I think it was so she could drink. Oh, I guess there was sex, too. But my father scolded her about drinking. 'The Curse of Our People.' My father would say, 'You can't keep doing that.' Granny's boyfriends probably just said, 'Have another, Fran!' She could drink with her boyfriends, so she had a lot of boyfriends."

My mother let her head fall back onto her pillows and twitched her nose. I no longer asked permission to slide out the nozzles of her oxygen tubes to dab the gobs of water that filled her nose, and she no longer felt—really, we didn't want to take the time—the need to say thank you. It was what we did to keep going.

"I don't know if Mother meant to kill herself," she said finally. "I think she got drunk and tried to pull a stunt. And it killed her."

My mother shut her eyes once more.

"Stupid, stupid, stupid," she said after a while. I lifted her shoulders slightly to puff up the pillows below, and after she fell back on them she lifted her eyes open.

"Suicide puts a fly in your head," she said. "It's always buzzing around. You never really get rid of it."

In the months that followed my grandmother's suicide, my mother went through her closets, packed up her clothes, and sifted through her small treasures, always alert for clues. Frances was too shrewd (or perhaps too experienced) to simply write down the names of men and their phone numbers in an address book. But my mother found initials and numbers written down on Drake Hotel cocktail napkins that were folded into some of her mother's purses, shoes, and scarves.

(Frances was shrewd but careless—or at least didn't care much if my grandfather discovered a napkin with numbers on the closet floor.)

"I found eight boyfriends," my mother told me in the ICU. "Current, active boyfriends," she emphasized. "The old ones she told me about must have been crumpled up and thrown away."

And in the years that followed, my mother made discreet contact with all eight of the men.

"All top-drawer guys," she remembered now. "A bank president. One of the heads of an ad agency." It was a name still on an agency today. "Even some kind of bishop." Episcopal. "A lovely man, really. He wore his collar and the purple shirt when we met in a coffee shop."

"So people would think you were planning the church picnic," I guessed, and my mother clamped her hand over her tubes to give a short snort.

"I don't think he wore it with Granny," she agreed. "Not for long. Then there was Eddie."

Not his real name. A railroad executive.

"I said that I wanted to talk to him, and he remembered having lunch with my mother and you," my mother recalled. "He suggested that I bring you along. We took the train out to Libertyville. He had a farm."

"I think I remember this!"

"He thought you'd like the horses."

"I did!"

"But we didn't see his wife. I think Granny's death caused some consternation in that house. He gave us a very lovely lunch out on his big lawn. Some cold cuts, bread, salad, and beer for us, and a little peanut butter and apple sandwich for you. He told me that he really cared for my mother. But he never misused the word 'love.' And he asked how my dad was doing. I told him he had gotten married just after Frances died, and that your dad and I weren't wild about it. He said, 'Give your dad a break, Patsy. He deserves to be happy. Frances is gone and she'd want that, too.' Really, a lovely man. You can meet good people under the most unlikely circumstances, can't you?"

My mother and I looked at each other a few moments (we knew we were running short of moments) before she went on.

"So I found eight of my mother's boyfriends," she said. "And six of them made passes at me. I guess they figured that if my mother would hop into bed with them . . ."

"They thought they were irresistible," I told her.

"They thought I was like my mother," my mother said, and I felt my eyes grow itchy and wet.

"My mother was so beautiful. So funny. I wanted to be with her. I wanted to *be* her. But I didn't want to wind up like her. All the wreckage she left. All the lies, going off like time bombs. All of the letdowns and crushed hearts. And then, one day, she got tired of herself and just floated away.

"It took me years to get that fly out of my head," said my mother. "Till I finally realized: I didn't want to be like my mother at all."

The whoosh of the door pulled open behind me signaled a new nurse, who held back behind a cart of monitors.

"You loved well and wrung every last breath out of life," I told my mother softly. "You've given me a hell of an inheritance."

My mother didn't like to keep a guest waiting. She had already lifted her head and a hand to let the nurse know she could roll forward.

"Pat, I'm Pamela," the nurse announced.

"And so very good to meet you, Pamela. This is my son."

We exchanged greetings and Pamela turned to wash her hands. Over the splashing and suds my mother called out, "You'll want to know my birthday, Pamela. It's August thirty-first. The year is too embarrassing.'"

"Then that's a good life, Pat," said the nurse. "You can be proud."

"I'm eighty-four!"

"We had a ninety-something man in here a while back," said Pamela. "Broke a leg doing the polka."

I told my mother I was going to pad out to use the restroom and head downstairs for coffee. Pamela rinsed and dried her hands with a great crinkling of paper towels and began to pull on blue hospital gloves. I leaned down to kiss my mother's forehead and she drew me close with a nod of her head.

"My mother can't help me now," she said quietly. "But if you ever need me—I'll break down a wall to get to you."

I plodded out into the hallway and all the bright lights and buzzers outside my mother's room blared and blinked like a carnival.

Mother: "I don't know why this is going on so long. I'm late for everything I guess."

15

We're singing through musicals my mother taught me to love (Fiorello now). She says, "I've seen so much talent in this world!"

My mother made smart remarks. I don't mean that she was witty or quotable, though she could be.

(A reporter writing a profile of my father, in the glory days of his comedy career, asked her, "What's it like to be married to the funniest man in Chicago?" My mother said with a cow-eyed, chorine shrug, "I wouldn't know.")

But she wasn't caustic, sarcastic, or snippy, the way wits are. She didn't strive to have people retell any zingers or wisecracks. Instead, she had a gift for saying the right thing to put someone at ease, make a point gently, or help someone laugh.

Just minutes after Ralph Newman was convicted in court, our family had to board an elevator to depart the federal courthouse in Chicago. When the steel doors parted we saw a familiar face inside: the gray-haired man who had been Juror Number 5.

He was courteous, and smiled at teary strangers. Then he looked away when he realized that he recognized us from the courtroom. *"Dear Amy: What do you say to the man you have just convicted and his family?"* We all stopped talking. The juror riveted his eyes to the upper corner of the elevator car, as if looking for a leak. We had another seventeen floors of close quarters and delicate silence until we reached the lobby, but my mother turned around to the man and spoke.

"Well, at least we all get to go home now and get some rest, don't we, sir?"

Back at her bedside, I told my mother, "That's the most amazing thing I ever heard anyone say in a tight situation. No politician, no statesman, no great writer, I think, ever topped that."

She lifted one eye wide open.

"I used to look at the jurors' faces. Didn't you?"

"Of course. Remember the nicknames we gave them? Popeye, Miss Sarah Vaughan, Turtle Man."

"He wasn't green. What was it?"

"Long tongue he couldn't keep cooped up in his mouth."

"Yes," she remembered. "Well, Number Five seemed so nice. He had very kind blue eyes. I could see him look at us, and he'd have to look away. He didn't want to hurt our family. He just had to do his duty. So I didn't want to hurt him."

My mother closed her eyes again.

"It was a sad, cold, raw, rotten day," she remembered. "So I thought: Let me try to give it a small kindness."

When sleep still didn't come my mother said, "Maybe we should tell jokes."

Jokes were not just laughing matters in our family. I knew from watching my father, knowing comics, and even from some of my own writing, that while jokes shouldn't be confused with coal mining, soldiering, or trash removal, they were work. If we did the job well (and just working hard wouldn't work; it had to be deft), the work produced laughs.

When my mother's mother died, the visitation was held at Mrs. Ahern's funeral home nearby. But when the priest arrived my mother looked around and figured out most of the mourners had beheld her mother in the casket for a moment—"Oh, Frances is still beautiful. Isn't she lovely now!"—then found their way to the kitchen in Mrs. Ahern's apartment above the funeral home.

My mother heard bursts of laughter from on high. She knew Mrs. Ahern had a few bottles in a cabinet, too, and picked up the house phone.

"Mrs. Ahern, is my husband there?"

"Oh dear, Ernest is here. But could you give him a moment? He's in the middle of the most marvelous joke."

"The priest wants to start prayers."

"He has his prayers, dear," Mrs. Ahern told her. "And Ernest has his jokes."

"And you know, that's where Frances would have been, too," said my mother.

Recalling those jokes was a way to retell and mark family history, too. Most families compile a personal joke catalog over the years, in which favorite stories are often conjured up by a phrase.

"The Astronaut Joke," I reminded my mother.

"The punch line," she remembered. "I had to spell it out."

"Astronaut is on top of his rocket. Countdown gets to T-minus three seconds and it starts raining," I prompted her. "They scrub the launch. It rains forty days and forty nights. Yet each morning the astronaut has to wake up and sit on the rocket."

"He's exhausted." My mother began to remember the story. "His wife says, 'Honey, let me go in your place. No one can tell who's in that silver suit. You sleep in.' So his wife sits on top of the rocket. It's raining cats and dogs. But then the sun breaks through."

"Five, four, three, two, one, liftoff!" I picked up the story. "The astronaut's wife begins pressing buttons, right?"

"She presses a black, unmarked button, and everything goes dark," my mother said. "She wakes up on a hospital table and a man in a white gown is pressing down on her bosoms. She says, 'What are you doing?' And the doctor says, 'Hang on, buddy. As soon as we get your b-a-l-l-s down, your p-r-i-c-k will pop out.'"

I laughed pretty much as I had when I was twelve years old. "I didn't know you even knew those words."

"Little boys think those words are state secrets. They're amazed their parents have heard them, too."

"Telling that joke to my friends made you the coolest mom. Dad thought spelling out the words made it even funnier. But only when you told it. He said it was like Jerry Lewis sneezing in the elevator."

"I was there for that! At the Chez Paree. Jerry just sneezed— and everyone laughed like he'd got a banana cream pie in his face. Just a sneeze! Not even one of his goofy Jerry sneezes. Some people try and try to be funny, and some people can just sneeze."

"Caroline had a good one the other night," I told her. "A mosquito landed in her wine. She picked it up with a finger, looked at it, and said, 'Spit it out! Spit it out!'"

My mother laughed hard enough to reach for a tissue.

"That's 'The Irishman With a Fly in His Beer,' isn't it?"

(Englishman, Frenchman, Irishman in a pub. Flies fall into their beers. The Englishman tells the bartender, "Another, please." The Frenchman flicks out his fly and just keeps drinking. The Irishman picks up his fly and hollers, "Spit it out! Spit it out, you little bastard!")

"Seeing a beautiful French lady say, 'Spit it out!' makes it funny," said my mother. "How does 'The Man on a Bridge in Belfast' go?"

It was one of our jokes when I was a teenager. Car bombs went off in Belfast every day, but our family there worried about coming to Chicago for a summer. Al Capone might gun them down.

"There's a man about to jump off a bridge in Belfast," I began.

"The Albert Bridge," my mother remembered.

"A priest runs down to shout, 'Don't jump, son! Jesus loves you.' 'But oh, Father,' says the man, 'I've done something turrrible. I killed me mah and me pah, I did.'"

My mother never liked my brogue (she thought I sounded like someone who auditioned for a Lucky Charms commercial—and wasn't hired), so she picked up the story.

"The priest tells him, 'Oh, son, don't worry. Jesus still loves you.'"

I dropped the brogue.

"'I killed my brother and sister, too,' the man said. 'And both my neighbors.' And the priest tells him, 'Jesus loves you no matter, son. Come down from that bridge and we'll pray. Hail Mary, full of grace.' And the man says, 'Oh, Father, I don't say Hail Mary. I'm a Protestant.' And the priest says, 'Protestant? Well jump, you dirty bastard!'"

My mother put a hand over her tubes to laugh.

"Remember 'Superman'?" I asked, and my mother made a vinegary little face.

"You gave it away already!" she pretended to grumble. "Two guys having a drink in the bar on top of the Hancock Building, right?"

"One of them gets up, opens the small window, and throws himself out. The other guy is amazed. But within a minute, he hears a great whistling noise, and the man pops back into the window. 'I bet you're really surprised,' he tells the other man.

'But this building is an architectural marvel. Know how it slopes at the bottom? You throw any object out of the top windows here, and the curve creates a wind that turns it around and brings it right back up.'"

"The other man has to try it, right?"

"Can't help himself," I agreed. "He crawls through the window and throws himself out. And he keeps dropping, dropping, dropping, until he finally hits the base of the building. Smashes into the sidewalk. And the bartender looks over at the man and says . . ."

I gave my mother a mock of a bow. I extended my palm as if motioning her to a favored seat, so she could say, "And the bartender says, 'Sometimes you're a real a-s-s-hole, Superman.'"

Setups and punch lines began to dash around my mind. But first I asked, "How much do you think it hurt Dad not to be big like Jerry Lewis?"

My father had worked as Jerry's straight man in a series of summer club dates, and appeared (briefly as a sneeze) in his movie *The Bellboy*.

My mother worked this over for a moment.

"We always blamed the drinking."

"Lots of big drinkers become big stars and cry for Oprah."

"Ernest was as funny as any of them," she said. "I swear. Nicer, too, with those merry brown eyes. We knew lots of people who'd drink as much—more—and never got drunk. Who knows why things work out the way they do?"

Tears came into her eyes, and disappeared just as quickly.

"It hurt him to feel discounted," I remembered. "We went into a drugstore once—he'd gotten a tiny little lamp for our grim little hotel room, and it didn't work—and the people behind the counter kept laughing and saying, 'What's the problem, Ernie? It was on sale. At that price you expect it to work, too?' He kept saying, 'But you bastards aren't hearing me. I bought a lamp and it doesn't light up. I thought I bought a lamp, not a doorstop,' and they kept laughing. We went back to the room—with the lamp—and turned on Johnny Carson. But I could see he was red-faced and crying under his glasses."

My mother put her hand over my elbow, then moved it over to find my hand.

"But he had great dignity at the end. Losing us was the hardest thing for your father. But he knew that I couldn't let us all go down on the *Titanic*. As much as it hurt, he knew it was the only way to save you."

I put both my hands over my mother's.

"For years I thought he died of sadness," she said. "All the rejections. All the booze. All the heartbreak. All the times he heard, 'Sorry, Ernie, but . . .' You know what I wound up thinking?" my mother told me. "Your father died because he couldn't help himself and he didn't want us going down, too. It was the last thing he could do for us and that's what he did."

We sat for a long moment, our hands folded, as the machines hooked into my mother blinked green and made ghastly organ music. I finally told my mother, "I've thought that for a long time too."

I had to move around, and stepped to the end of her bed.

"Dad always said, 'Any joke that begins, 'A minister, a priest, and a rabbi . . .'"

"You know who's gonna get the punch line," said my mother. She squirmed her shoulder and I came over to lift her farther up on her pillow.

"The richest man in town is about to die," she began. "He's an atheist. But he calls a minister, a priest, and a rabbi to his bed and says, 'You're the only men I can trust. I'm giving you each an envelope with a million dollars in cash, and trust you to put it with me in my casket.'

"Well, the man dies that night. The minister, priest, and rabbi all leave their envelopes in his casket. They decide to share a cab back to their houses of worship. The minister says, 'Brothers, I'm feeling a little guilty. I took the envelope back to my church, saw how badly the roof leaks on our congregation, and—well—I took out ten thousand dollars to repair it.'

"Then the priest says, 'I, too, have a confession. I got back to my church and a nun told me that unless we came up with fifteen thousand dollars, we'd have to close the soup kitchen in our basement. So I opened the envelope, saw all that cash, and told myself, "The man who gave me all this money is with God now." So I took out fifteen thousand to keep our soup kitchen running.' "

On that line I knew to ask, "And the rabbi?"

"The rabbi gets angry," said my mother. "He tells the minister and priest, 'Gentlemen, I'm shocked. *Shocked*. We gave that man our personal, solemn promises as men of faith to put his money in his casket.'

" 'But, Rabbi,' the minister asks, 'weren't you tempted? Just a little?' The priest asks, 'To take just a little of that money from your envelope to do something good, instead of let it just rot in that rich man's grave?'

"And the rabbi says, 'Of course, brothers. But he trusted us. I guarantee you: my personal check for one million dollars is in that casket!' "

Someone had opened the door to the room but held back behind the privacy curtain.

"I am sorry to break up the party," he announced, and my mother recognized his voice.

"Oh, Derek," she said. "You must have been away for a few days. Meet my son."

Derek seemed to be in his mid-thirties, with a dapper vandyke beard and a euphonious accent.

"Derek is from Poland," my mother said by way of introduction, "and has given me permission to call him by his first name."

"No one can say my last name," he explained, and when I asked him to help me, I stumbled, too.

"It's all right. Not even Polish people can say it, and practically everyone from Chicago is Polish."

"The president?" I asked, and Derek didn't need as much as a moment to have an answer.

"If they trace back far enough," he said. "Washington, Jefferson, too."

I told my mother I would excuse myself for a bathroom break and a coffee run.

"When I return," I told her, "Cousin Megan's joke."

"The young Irish girl who's been out all night?" she asked. "I don't know if Derek wants to hear our old family material."

"Oh, I love jokes," said Derek. "We don't hear enough of them here."

My mother lifted her eyes when she heard me return, softly.

"Darling, have you heard from Chuck recently?"

"Father Chuck?"

A Franciscan priest, Charles Faso, was a family friend.

"An e-mail now and then," I told her. "A few phone calls. He travels so much: retreats and conferences. He takes people on Holy Land cruises."

Chuck was dashing, now in his seventies. He sang beautifully, had a light, graceful step when he danced, and looked elegant in his brown, homespun Franciscan robe. When he came to my mother and Ralph Newman's apartment for a party before Christmas Eve mass, her gal pals would see such a conspicuously debonair man and mutter to one another (Chuck had heard it all of his priestly life), "What a waste."

My mother would greet Chuck in his Franciscan robes and announce, "Now there's a man who knows how to dress for Christmas."

What she said now was, "Chuck always had so many good jokes. You should call him."

"Right now."

"If he has a few moments," she said, "it would be nice to see him."

There was a slender band of summer light burning at the bottom of the window shade and I figured that Father Chuck must be at prayer.

There was a clock on the wall but the room was usually too dark to see it. I wore a watch but rarely lifted my sleeve, and didn't note the time in small numbers at the top of my phone. I see now: I didn't want time to pass. Even the meals had become unvarying and indistinguishable. I went downstairs for coffee and an apple, whatever the hour. My mother could no longer swallow Jell-O, so every few hours—by now, it was even on demand—a nurse brought her a small paper cup of a lemon Italian ice.

"Dessert whenever I want," she said. "Breakfast, lunch, and dinner. I'm living large now."

Mother: what time is it? Me: 6:30. Her: oh let's raise the curtains on the city we love.

16

I tell my mother, "You'll never stop teaching me."
She said, "Well don't blame me for everything."

"Oh, fish sticks," said my mother. "What did I ever really teach you?"

I didn't think long.

"How to be kind. How to be courteous. How to work hard. How to dress."

"Not always," she pointed out.

"I was rebelling," I reminded her. "How to love animals."

"I tried to teach you how to roller-skate. Remember? But we were living in San Francisco."

We laughed to recall the two of us on wheels, when skates were made of steel, rolling maybe twenty feet before we reached a steep hill and stopped so fast we saw sparks.

"You said, 'I guess I thought the hills were all on postcards,'" I remembered. "Took me years to appreciate how funny that was. You know"—it came into my mind—"you taught me about art."

My mother shook her head slightly.

"I like it. I don't know it," she said.

"You taught me to open my eyes," I told her. "That's how you begin."

My mother had grown up beholding Chicago's Art Institute along South Michigan Avenue, a great white whale of a Beaux Arts building built for a World's Fair, and guarded by two bronze lions (who wear evergreen wreaths during the holidays). But she didn't venture inside until she was about nineteen, working temp office jobs during the day and in clubs at night, when she would walk over to Michigan Avenue to stop in a coffee shop before she caught the bus to the Near North Side.

"I just wandered in one summer day," she remembered now. "The place was so cool, with white marble, and you could walk from room to room, or just sit, look, and dream. It was like a vacation. There was Gauguin," she remembered. "There was Van Gogh. Outside were the buses and the trains and the police sirens. But inside, there was Tahiti. There was a street in Paris. There was a ballet dancer in her dressing room, rolling on her socks. Or was she taking them off? Degas, Lautrec, and Dufy."

I propped my elbow on a pillow to ask, "What did you like about them?"

My mother paused and let out a breath.

"The color they saw," she said. "They saw the same things, but with different colors. To put that in our eyes, too—amazing."

"I loved going to the Art Institute with you."

"I made sure to promise you a hot fudge sundae at the end."

I lifted myself up a little more on the heel of my hand.

"But it's like you planned," I told her. "I'd forgotten the sundae. But I remember a lot of the paintings, and show them to our daughters now. I remember walking from room to room with you."

I remember the slap and squeak of our snow boots on smooth floors in the hush of the halls, and the smell of our wet collars as we strolled through the Paris, Venice, and Tokyo on the walls.

"You can go all around the world," my mother told me. "In just a few steps."

Some of the world's best-known paintings hang in the Art Institute, and my mother brought me face to face with them time and again.

"It's like what they say about Disneyland," she told me once as we stood in front of *A Sunday on La Grande Jatte*. "You can't see it all in a day. Seurat put so much in here, didn't he?"

The lady with the red umbrella walking with a child in a white frock; the girl sitting on her legs in the grass, holding flowers—are they a gift, or a wish?; the funny little gray monkey arching his back at the little brown dog who leaps past; the lady knitting, the man sprawled on his elbows, the top-hatted man with a slender cane—is she with one, both, or neither?; the sun painting gold on the grass, white tissue clouds wafting through the shade, the trees wooly with green leaves, the lake dappled blue with dots of white and brown and yellow.

"See all those millions of tiny dots?" my mother asked. I leaned forward and squinted. "It's called pointillism," she explained. "Each little dot is just a speck. But they each touch our eyes. The dots make things move, even while they stay still. The dots are like molecules. Put them together, and it's life. Isn't that amazing?"

My mother raised a gloved hand to point toward the back of the painting's eye, where there were boaters, sunbathers, and a man playing a horn.

"If you moved the painting to the right," she said, "the man with the horn would be in the center. The couple with beautiful posture, and the two top hats—almost matching, aren't they?—wouldn't be there at all. Maybe just the little girl skipping on that side. But move it to the left, would we see the lake? Or the man with the horn? Or see—I'm just noticing it now, and I've seen this painting a hundred times—the four folks paddling the boat? You'd think Seurat would put them all in the same position, but they're all slightly—even just an inch or two— different. The boaters, the bathers, the couple curled under the man with the horn, all just kind of looking into the cool blue lake. Each of them could be a painting all by themselves, too, couldn't they? There's a painting in every person, isn't there?"

Grant Wood's *American Gothic* hung in another room: the slender, slightly pinched faces, pasty as dough, the high white collars, the long, sharp tines of the pitchfork.

"He looks like Uncle Waltie," I told my mother.

"A little," she agreed. "But that sure isn't Auntie Chris. She doesn't get that buttoned up to go to church. Look at that house behind the couple," she went on. "So neat and sturdy, isn't it? And that worn red barn. I think they've worked hard," said my mother. "Those harsh, Iowa winters, when people had to walk everywhere, and they didn't have snowplows. Or indoor plumbing or electric stoves. That pitchfork is there because in those days, they didn't have those big machines they do now to plant and cut and pick all the corn and stuff."

(No one in our family had had much to do with farming since the Great Potato Blight. Our understanding was imprecise.)

"When you begin to look at art," she said, "you see it every day. Not just in a museum. You see it on farms, streets, and alleys. When we're on the El and see people leaning out of their windows, look at their faces. Grant Wood could have painted them, too. He did, in a way, when he painted this couple. They might have moved from the farm to Chicago, if their crops went bad, and now they lean out of their window on a hot summer night, dreaming of the farm."

Edward Hopper's *Nighthawks* was in another room. I kept going back to it, drawn like a fly to its shrill, yellow, all-night light. There was the white-capped server, dipping below the counter—for what? The red-haired, red-lipped, red-dressed woman staring dully, the man with the downturned beak of his fedora and hard-set face (Night Hawk himself?), the stools, like squeaking lily pads, below the counter, the silver-gray coffee urns blinking back light, the empty street, eerie with a quiet yellow glow.

"Where's the door?" my mother asked.

I looked.

"I don't see it."

"You don't see it. Or there isn't any?"

"There's got to be a door." I got a little huffy. "How else do they get in there?"

"That's good. Then why doesn't Mr. Hopper show it?"

"It's, like, in the back."

"Wouldn't an all-night diner have the door in front? On the street?"

That stopped me for a moment.

"Maybe they were born there," I proposed.

"Maybe," said my mother. "Or they're trapped there, just smoking and eating grilled cheese sandwiches. *Forever.*"

"I know," I told her. "James Bond could parachute on top, blow a hole in the roof, and get them all out." I began to sing. "Duh-duh-duh-duh, da-da-da!"

I invoked James Bond to explain a lot of phenomena and purported miracles; it saved time I could otherwise spend learning facts. This made my mother wince, but teachers, rabbis, and priests would often say, "What an imaginative young man!"

I leaned a little closer toward the painting. My mother leaned down to draw her head next to mine.

"Can't you almost hear the coffee cups clink?"

"It's so bright. You could, like, almost read a newspaper by it."

"Artists create their own light," my mother told me.

My mother and I stood in front of Cézanne's *The Basket of Apples*, spilled all over a tilted table. "Life works that way sometimes," she told me. "You put all your apples in a basket, then the basket tips."

Caillebotte's *Paris Street; Rainy Day*. "Imagine if you had just one day in Paris, and it rained," said my mother. "'Oh no,' you'd say. But look at this painting, and you'd see: you're lucky. Rain makes the city quiet and personal."

And Van Gogh's *The Bedroom*. "Do you think Van Gogh really made his bed every day? Or just for the painting, because he knew his mother would see it?"

My mother lifted her eyes and asked me now, "Do you remember the first time you saw *At the Moulin Rouge*?"

"I'm not sure about the first time," I told her. "I remember seeing it over and over."

I remember seeing the short, dapper, bearded man, whom I would discover was Henri de Toulouse-Lautrec, sitting with others at a small table at what looks like a loud club. One of the women at the table has a painted white face.

"'Like a ghost,' you said," my mother remembered. "Not a clown. That's what most children would say."

"I was different," I told her now.

"And I was worried. I asked Auntie Chris, 'What's wrong with him, that he sees ghosts, not clowns?' And Auntie Chris said, 'Oh, you know, so much has happened to the poor kid, he's probably crying inside.' Then she said, 'Wait: there's a cartoon character that's a ghost. That's all it is.'"

"Casper," I agreed, and my mother and I laughed.

"I can still see another woman in there, though," I told her. "She's dancing. Another white face, shading blue. But the people ignore the dancers."

"And they just keep dancing, right?" My mother shut her eyes. "The dancers dance, whether people pay attention or not. Do you think that's why we loved Toulouse so much? So many places that your dad worked—everybody worked hard, and then people wouldn't pay attention. Dad wanted to say, 'If you want to talk, stay home. No cover charge.' But he couldn't."

"He could say it just once," I told her now.

The two of us would stand for minutes in front of *Equestrienne (At the Cirque Fernando)*, eyeing the horse handler with a whip, the red-wigged rider facing him, the horse bucking his muzzle under to run.

"It's a working horse," my mother said. "Just like the girls at the Moulin Rouge were working girls. Just like Toulouse was a working artist. No wonder he loved them."

My mother and I shared Lautrec like a hobby. He became our family artist. We recognized the world of laughter and bright lights, exhaustion and dark corners, that he painted with such vivid tenderness.

She brought home large art books from the library, with yellowed leaves holding fading Lautrec prints. We went to a huge bookstore in the Loop and brought home books printed in French on smooth, slick paper. We pored over columns of French, trying to pick out recognizable words.

"Henri was just thirty-six when he died," my mother said.

"And yet, all these pictures. He painted like he knew he had a lot of work to do while he could."

She read thick English-language art books and biographies, marking paragraphs for me with curlicue scraps of yellow paper.

"He was a dwarf," my mother explained. "He had an accident as a child, and it never healed. He may have had a disease. So Toulouse had a regular body, but short legs, like a child. He was born into a noble family, and in those days, people thought bad things happened because you did something wrong. So he was distant from his family, and found a home in nightclubs. The ladies became his friends. They were probably distant from their families, too. They all threw themselves into their work, and Henri's was painting. I think they looked out for each other."

We kept a yellow scrap parked permanently at a print of a picture called *La Toilette*: another of Henri's auburn-haired women, who sits in a pile of petticoats, a boot wiggling on her right leg, a tin tub just ahead of her.

"She's getting ready to take a bath," I once announced.

"Or did she just?" asked my mother.

"She looks tired. She wants to take a bath and go to bed. Look at her shoulders."

"She's tired," said my mother. "But she has to freshen up and still do something else. Another show. Another chore."

One day I asked, "Did you ever feel like that?" and my mother shook her head and spoke softly.

"Who hasn't? Any mother has felt like that," she said. "Dead tired, and a whole day or night ahead."

My mother had a story for Jane Avril, the woman with gold hair and a high kick who was the star dancer at the Moulin Rouge. It was lyrical if a little historically shaky.

"Oh, how Henri loved Jane. And she loved him. But not in the way he wanted."

"Because he was a dwarf?"

"Henri had lots of problems. He drank too much. He was very unhappy. Being so short probably made him feel shortchanged in life, don't you think? He was lovely to spend time with in the Moulin Rouge. Coming home to him? Different matter.

"But Henri could paint her," continued my mother. "He could capture her. No other man could do that for her."

My mother had shut her eyes and found a few steady breaths. Derek had entered silently behind us. I think word had spread across shifts; nurses and technicians had begun to wrench the glass door open softly.

My mother lifted her eyes half open.

"*Nighthawks*," she said. "The people in the diner. Do you think they'll ever get out? Maybe I'll see them someday. . . ."

Her voice trailed off.

"They don't seem in a hurry to leave," I told her. "Outside— who knows? Cold and dark. The wind blows. But inside, it's bright and warm."

"I'll bet the food is terrible. Like hospital food."

"They're with each other," I said, and tightened my hand around my mother's. "Just like I'm in no hurry for us to leave here."

"But you've got things to do, baby," my mother said as Derek cleared his throat and approached with soft steps.

I don't know how we'll get through these next few days. And, I don't want them to end.

17

If we only truly realized how little time we have . . .

"We have to thank artists, don't we? They help us see the world differently."

"But you did that for me," I told my mother.

I remembered one winter night: it must have been December. Snow nipped our faces, ice crackled under our boots, and I swiped the back of a glove under my raw nose.

We crossed Michigan Avenue at Randolph Street, where my mother worked as a secretary in an ad agency, and walked by the broad stone stairs of the old central Chicago Public Library.

It must have been rush hour—buses backed up, motors thrumming, people trudging quick as they could hit their footing in the flurries. I remember the skirl of police traffic whistles, corner by corner, and the dings of Salvation Army bell ringers in thin black coats, snow flocking on their collars. My mother put nickels and dimes in my hands, which I'd let slide into their red kettles.

"Merry Christmas! Merry Christmas!"

There was a man on the stairs with his hand out. He had a worn red Indian-print blanket around his shoulders, and a tatty brown beard, where flakes fell, melted, and glistened. His brown hair was matted, frosted, and whipped by snow. I was ten or eleven and he looked like the man who lived in a cave in about a hundred children's stories.

"He looks biblical," said my mother.

It was cold but she stopped so she could fish for one more coin in her purse. She held it out to him and let it drop softly into his bare hand.

"You must be cold, dear," said my mother.

The man just looked up. His eyes looked flat, glassy, and gray.

"Get some soup or something," my mother told him. "There are a couple of places downstairs in the train station, where it's warm."

The man just kept looking. My mother snapped her purse open again, and found a dollar.

"Keep this in your hand," she told him. "They just want to know you can pay."

He folded his fingers over the bill and the coin and grunted. Then he began to growl. He stamped his heels on the stairs and snarled angry, indecipherable words.

My mother took my hand tightly and we walked quickly away toward the bells and lights on State Street.

"You were just trying to help," I told my mother.

"The poor man was hurt," she said. "He probably sleeps on a bench. Or in the street. He's tired. He's probably hungry. He's probably sick. He's probably embarrassed, too, don't you think? To be seen like that. But if he wants some soup, he'll get it," she said, as we tramped on. "We're so lucky in life. He doesn't have to say thank you."

"Why is that man like that? What happened?" I asked. This was a little before quite so many people lived on the street in America, and before most of us walked past them without much notice.

"Who knows?" said my mother. "So many things can happen in life. Look at him and think: He was once a little baby whose mother loved him."

I asked my mother now, "Do you remember the night near Christmas when we saw a homeless man on the steps of the library? You gave him a dollar. He got angry. You said, 'Remember, he was once a little baby whose mother loved him.'"

My mother turned her hands up slightly from her covers.

"I said that all the time. I must have said that a hundred times. You just remember that once?"

I tried to pedal back.

"Maybe a few more times, too . . ."

"Haven't you found that out?" my mother asked. "You tell your children something a hundred times. You're lucky if they remember it once. You tell them hundreds of things. You're lucky if they remember one or two. Dos, don'ts, count for almost nothing. All they remember is what you do. Whether you want them to or not."

I took my mother's hand. I rubbed a purple-blue splotch that had been inflicted by a needle or a tube. Her veins, which were always thin and hard to pinpoint and puncture, seemed to hide under her bones now.

"Right now, I wish I could remember a few more things you said," I told her.

"You will," she said. "And you'll get them all mixed up with things other people said. Those are the stories you'll tell your children, and they'll become their stories."

Rosemary peered around the glass door and rapped it with her hand.

"Visitors," she announced.

Father Chuck managed to look debonair in a short-sleeved red sport shirt and stretchy black slacks. He carried a small black satchel.

"Patti, I'm sorry I'm not in my costume!"

"It's just wonderful to see you, dear."

Chuck lifted her hand and brushed it against his lips. She squeezed his hand back.

They spent a moment—but really, just one—talking about his travels and family. My mother didn't have the breath for much delay.

"Chuck, dear, I need your help," she told him.

Chuck had opened his black satchel and removed a book of sacraments. He draped vestment ribbons over his sport shirt and took my mother's hand again.

My mother had spent most of her life in rebellion against her church (like a lot of American Catholics, I think it's safe to say). She wouldn't miss mass at Easter and on Christmas Eve; she would slip into churches in times of stress and testing to utter prayers and light candles. But she was everlastingly angry at her church—not because of priestly abuses, the subordination of women, or Vatican bank scandals, but because she had felt cast out of her faith when she married the man she loved (and then two more Jewish men, to compound her disobedience).

When we went to Chuck's midnight mass, at a small church west of the Loop, we'd sit with him in the basement afterwards over espresso and delectable little Italian cookies. He put on a great show on Christmas Eve, with a choir of unearthly voices and a baby Jesus (a doll from a department store, he once acknowledged) lifted up in a straw-filled basket. My mother's eyes were often still enchanted and glassy when she spoke of it.

"Such a beautiful, beautiful service, Chuck. Just lovely."

"You know, Patti, we have one of these every Sunday. . . ."

"Too much time has passed. And I'm still upset."

"All of that's changed, you know," Chuck would tell her. "These days, we're just glad when people get married." And my mother would laugh that away.

I sometimes spoke up for the church from which my mother felt estranged.

"Every shithole in the world I go to," I told her, "you see them. Every place I see filled with suffering, misery, and death, one day you look up and see a group of nuns or priests in the rubble. They try to help where no one else dares to go."

"Well, they have a lot to make up for," she liked to say.

But now my mother put up a hand. Father Chuck took her fingers lightly between his palms.

"You have brought so many people so many blessings, Patti," he said. "But I guess all of us can stand to say, 'Oh, God, I am heartily sorry for having offended you . . . ,'" and my mother picked up his words in a low, steady voice.

"'I detest all my sins because of your just punishment, but most of all because they offend you, my God . . .'"

I heard the words and knew I could stand to say them, too, but stepped softly out of the room.

Old friend, Fr Chuck, comes by to recite Act of
Contrition w/ my mother. We love him. My mother
has nothing to be—

—contrite about. But she is typically gracious in
saying it w/ Fr. Chuck.

18

City is cool, bright, & lovely this morning. My mother touches a splash of sunlight w/ her fingers. "Hello, Chicago!"

When I returned, Mr. Washington had rolled in his respiration cart and my mother looked refreshed.

"Why don't we watch a movie?" she suggested.

I fumbled for the remote on her bedside stand and began to flick through channels. There were things exploding and people snarling (and that was just the news).

"Remember what we saw the other night, Mr. Washington?" my mother asked as he noted numbers and folded tubing.

"Sure do," he said. "Never forget."

"A man—a Viking or something, he was dressed like a mastodon, all hairy with tusks coming out of his helmet—was having his way with a woman."

"And not in the ordinary way," Mr. Washington added.

"And how long did the two of you watch this disgusting display?" I asked, and my mother and Mr. Washington grinned.

"We couldn't find the remote," she explained. "It was under

a flap of the covers or something. Meanwhile, this whole scene went on and on. The man was using a whaddya call it—some kind of paddle."

"An oar," he suggested.

"Yeow," I heard myself say.

"It wasn't *It Happened One Night*, was it, Mr. Washington? It was more like assault and battery."

Mr. Washington shook his head back and forth.

"That young lady wanted no part of it."

"We did switch channels—Mr. Washington had to find the remote for me—but there was nothing we could watch, really, was there?"

"It gets pretty grim, late at night," he said, and offered biblical words of explanation. "Lots of blood and pillaging."

My mother raised her head from the pillow.

"You know," she said, "they should have a channel showing things that people stuck in a hospital would really like to see."

"You don't like their Wellness channel?"

That was the in-house hospital channel that droned with pan flute music, babbling waterfalls, fluffy polar bear cubs, and tender sunsets. Now and then a severely slender woman with her hair pulled back, Georgia O'Keeffe–style, would appear and perform prolonged, elastic stretches.

My mother made a sour little face and shrugged.

"Most of us aren't in a position to do much yoga," she said. "And that music drives you crazy."

"They have all the news channels," I pointed out.

"The news is depressing."

"Don't I know . . ."

"All those important things they talk about," said my mother. "It's hard to hear when I don't think I'll be around for them."

I ignored her remark. Or rather, I knew by now that my mother was only telling the truth and had begun to figure she deserved only the truth in return; or when that was just too painful to hear myself say, at least silence. My mother went on.

"They should show movies that people in the hospital would want to see," she suggested. "Movies you want to see over and over because they make you smile."

"*Blazing Saddles?*"

My mother wrinkled her nose.

"The campfire scene?"

"People on bedpans should love it."

My mother laughed and jiggled the oxygen tubes out of her nostrils.

"I was thinking more like . . ."

I leaned down to help resettle her tubing, and remembered the way she used to mop my hot forehead with her cool and beautiful hands when I was a sick little boy.

"*Singin' in the Rain,*" she said. "You love that, don't you?"

"'Make 'em laugh, make 'em laugh,'" I began, and my mother chimed in with her (even when strained through clotted tubing) vastly superior singing voice. "'Don'tcha know everyone wants to laugh. . . .'" We did for several seconds.

"Amazing," she said, "wasn't it? The dummy, falling behind the sofa, dancing up the wall." She closed her eyes again for a moment.

"*Roman Holiday,*" she said. "Gregory Peck."

"All reporters look like Gregory Peck," I assured her, then added, "Audrey Hepburn."

"Remember the haircut scene? Audrey Hepburn gets her hair cut short so people won't know she's a princess, and she wound up making that short hair the image of a princess. What about *Anatomy of a Murder?*"

"It's no comedy."

"But so well done. And lots of great little touches, like in a great painting. When Jimmy Stewart hesitates to say 'panties'? It's hilarious, isn't it? Someone says, 'I think the French have a word for that,' and Jimmy Stewart says, 'They usually do . . .'"

"*Some Like It Hot*?" I wondered.

"Oh yes. Those boys are both so funny, aren't they? And Marilyn. Funny and beautiful."

"Devastating combination," I agreed.

"Oh, and *Casablanca*," said my mother. "How could we possibly forget *Casablanca*?"

"Round up the usual suspects," I told her.

"*The Germans wore gray; you wore blue.*"

"I came for the waters."

"But we're in a desert!"

"I . . . I . . . I was misinformed."

"Well. I'm shocked. *Shocked.*"

"We'll always have Paris," I told my mother, and I'm sure we stopped for a moment for the word to ring between us. Paris stood in for a recollection of laughs, losses, fears, and delights, squashed into seconds.

"You do the thinking for both of us," she said, slowly, softly, finally.

"The problems of two little people don't amount to a hill of beans. . . ." I told her in return. My mother brightened.

"The 'La Marseillaise' scene," she remembered. "'Play "La Marseillaise." *Play "La Marseillaise"!*' The hooker in the bar gets all teary, bless her."

"*Aux armes, citoyens!*"

"A lot of people still think she should have stayed with Rick."

"Well, he told her: where he was going, what he'd be doing— 'You can't be a part of that.'"

My mother put down the heels of her hands and tried to sit forward.

"I don't know why people say that she really loved Rick. She flew off with Victor."

"Yes, but only after Rick did the thinking for both of them," I reminded her, and my mother shook her head.

"Rick did the thinking that she *knew* he would. He was a great guy for a week in Paris—or a weekend in Casablanca. But he'd never be the kind of man who'd look forward to coming home. That was Laszlo. He led the Nazis on a wild-goose chase because he was fighting for his home. Ilsa gives Victor a look when he leads the band to sing 'La Marseillaise.' Do you remember?"

I didn't.

"See it again," she advised. "You'll see what I mean."

(Months later, I did; she was right.)

"Believe you me," said my mother. "If Ilsa had stayed with Rick, before long he'd be hanging out at the bar with his buddies. He'd leave Sam with the club and Ilsa upstairs and just run off with Louis to the French foreign legion."

"Sounds like you knew him."

My mother just smiled and said, "A few people like him."

I finally remembered that I had downloaded *42*, Brian Helgeland's film about Jackie Robinson's entry into major league baseball. I had written a book about Jackie Robinson, and appreciated the challenge of compressing years of history and experience into a compelling and coherent two hours. I liked the film, and thought my mother, who knew the story, would be lifted up to cheer for Jackie Robinson.

One of the film's producers had called me about Wendell Smith, the sportswriter who had roomed with Jackie Robinson when he broke in with the Dodgers. Wendell was doing a late-night sports show in Chicago by the time I came along, on which my father would come in to do car commercials. At that point in their lives, Wendell and my father—a black man and a Jew—were agreeably similar in appearance: slightly stocky, a little dandy, each with a pencil-thin moustache.

Wendell might have been a little lighter in complexion than my father.

"How are you, son of mine?" he'd josh, and tousle my hair, when my father brought me in on Friday nights. "You tell your momma the check is in the mail." And I remember their deep laughs and falling asleep against my father's shoulder when they'd tell stories and have a quick drink—or three—across the street.

My mother and I watched a scene early in the movie, one with André Holland, the young actor who played Wendell, who is slender to the point of balletic.

"Wendell Smith?" my mother asked. I nodded.

"Well, that young man is a wonderful actor," she said. "But the only thing that looks like Wendell is the moustache."

"Wendell was actually a college athlete. It was right after the war. He and dad were both skinnier then. Writing puts on pounds," I told her, and thumped my own stomach. My mother rolled her eyes.

"Telling stories with your father over drinks, round after round, puts on pounds."

We watched a scene in which a mature, athletic man with round shoulders and just a fringe of hair is shaken out of the satiny sheets he shares with an unnamed blonde in Beverly Hills by a late-night phone call. He tells Harrison Ford's Branch Rickey, "Nice guys finish last."

"Leo Durocher?" my mother asked. I nodded once more.

"Oh, I remember him, too."

During my auntie Marion's marriage (her third) to Charlie

Grimm, the old Cubs first baseman and former manager, they had picked up Leo when he landed in Chicago to become manager of the Cubs, late in his career, and often spent nights with him closing down Eli's on Chicago Avenue.

"Who's the actor?"

"Christopher Meloni."

"He's good. He's *handsome*," she added. "You know, so many people think of Leo just when he was a cranky old guy."

"Remember when I was a kid, and you'd let me walk down to Tribune Tower after dinner to get the early edition of the paper? Leo would be in front of his apartment building. He'd talk to anybody. He was charming and funny."

"His wife would send him out to smoke," my mother remembered. She had turned her attention back to the film and we were holding hands and onto the next scene when she told me, "Well, in his day, I tell you, Leo was a very vital and attractive man."

Thanks for all kind messages. We're watching 42 (movie), cherishing every second of normalcy. Cherish yr mother tonight too.

Watching 42, mother remembers Leo Durocher made passes at her twice: "Once as a Dodger, once as a Cub." Who's the all-star?

19

A thought tonight for all who are in pain. We must be stronger than our fears.

My mother had to battle to breathe now. Her lung-and-a-half was scarred and flimsy, but she was also scared. She knew by now—we both did—that at any moment she would gasp for air and not be able to hold it. She would, in a way, drown right there in her hospital bed, despite all the machines and nurses and tubes running in and out of her like a subway map. I don't think she was scared of death (although she'd be entitled) so much as the pain and indignity.

Derek had come back on duty. My mother gasped and wheezed as he put a full mask over her nose and mouth. The full mask didn't poke and chafe her nose, like the tubes, but could make her feel trapped. Her breaths sputtered.

"Slow, slow, slow," he told her slowly.

Derek put the palm of his hand on my mother's back and rubbed, with a soft, light hand, as if he were trying to keep a butterfly on his fingers.

"We are here, Pat," he told her. "Slow down and just breathe."

My mother fell back on her pillows. I wiped the sheen on her forehead with the cuff of my shirt.

"Thank you so much, Derek," she said.

Mother asks, "Will this go on forever?" She means pain, dread. "No." She says, "But we'll go on forever. You & me." Yes.

20

In middle of nights like this, my knees shake as if there's an earthquake. I hold my mother's arm for strength—still.

When my mother closed her eyes, I stepped out to call my wife. I could hear that my mother's one good lung had become as fragile as a rice paper lantern. She coughed, racking, scratching, and hacking, gasps and rasps that were agonizing even to hear.

I put my shoulder lightly to her forehead. I put a hand gently on her back, holding her like she'd once held me through fevers, flus, and whooping cough. She shivered—we both did—in all the bleeps, buzzers, and blinking lights.

The glass door of her room in the intensive care unit was pulled open.

"Mary," my mother cawed and wheezed when she saw she had lived to see another shift. "Sweet Mary."

Mary was trim, blond, and practical.

"How are you doing, Patricia?"

Mary's hands were fast, smart, and kind. She pulled my mother up carefully from below her pale shoulders. She turned the flat, hot pillows behind my mother's head cool and fluffy with two quick punches. She dabbed the plump drops of condensation from my mother's oxygen tubing and resettled it inside her nose. And then she smoothed back my mother's fringe of hair with her fingers.

My mother caught her breath (you don't understand that phrase until you see someone wheeze and wonder if they can grab enough air to breathe again) and used it to say, "Mary is the loveliest person. She went to St. Scholastica, didn't you, Mary?"

Mary smiled.

"My mother went to Immaculata," I told her. "On Irving. It's condos now. After she was thrown out of another school for trying on a nun's habit."

"No!" said Mary, who must have seen a lot, but not that. "She didn't tell me that!"

"We were just curious girls," said my mother. Her face was getting a calmer color and her voice was getting stronger. "Dolores Gonnella and I."

"Did you want to be a nun?"

"Oh no, dear. It was already far too late for that."

Now it was Mary who coughed as she laughed. She switched out one of the clear bags above the bed and tapped the screen of one of the beeping medical appliances.

"Mary, dear . . . ," my mother began.

"I'll be right back," Mary assured her, and I kissed my mother and excused myself, too.

Mary had wheeled one of the bedpan carts outside of my mother's room. I'd shut the door but kept my voice soft.

"Thank you, Mary."

"Your mom's doing great."

"This is hard."

"She's doing great."

Is this how it happens? I asked, with audible italics, and Mary held her answer for a moment to put a hand lightly on my sleeve.

"Yes," she told me. "And it's hard. But she's doing great."

While my mother busied herself on the bedpan, I paced outside remembering the years she'd read *Pinocchio* or *Winnie-the-Pooh* to little-boy-me in a repertory of voices while my face purpled on the toilet seat (a mother's love indeed). I returned calls to a couple of people, keeping my voice low outside of my mother's room, but trying to speak above the ghastly organ chorus of beeping machines that bleated up and down the intensive care unit.

Mary whooshed the door open and motioned me back inside. She had lowered the headrest of my mother's bed and dimmed a light. My mother's eyes were closed and I tried to step lightly.

"Baby?" she called softly.

"I'm back," I told her. "I'm here."

I held her hand. She lifted her eyes to half-mast and just said, "Nice," before they closed again.

Wake up, see my hands shaking. Mother holds them, murmurs, "Goodnight Sweet Prince." Morphine, but no sleep for her.

21

Family joins me today. Maybe they'll help me to be strong. My mother showed me how that's done, come to think of it.

The night before my mother had her first cancer surgery we went to dinner at a restaurant near her apartment, and during dessert something stuck in her throat. She began to cough ferociously and bent below the table. I held her shoulders. She gasped and shuddered.

"I don't mind dying," my mother told us when at last she could finally sit up and breathe. "I just don't want to lose my dignity."

We walked back to her apartment. It was a cold, slushy night and my mother knew how to plot the best path through a succession of snug, dry hotel lobbies along the way.

"I could leave the Singapore or Mister Kelly's in one outfit," she remembered, "freshen up and change in the Drake. I want to show Elise a ladies' room," she told us. My wife and I had just one daughter then, who was about three. "It's a beauty," she assured us.

How could we refuse what seemed like it could be a coughing grandmother's last request?

So my wife, mother, and daughter went into the posh ladies' room while my mother's husband and I waited on a bench outside, left to imagine what marvels we might have missed, condemned to life's men's rooms. Hot towels? Toe massages? Champagne cocktails?

When our family emerged, Elise giggled and my wife's eyes shined. She said my mother had patted silky creams into Elise's little pink hands, swabbed them with perfumed soaps, and dried them with cottony cream-puff towels. What did my mother tell her granddaughter, who was adopted from a Chinese orphanage, with what she thought might be one of her last breaths?

"Never be afraid to go into a classy place, baby. Remember: you belong."

When my mother's family first came to Chicago, there were still NO IRISH NEED APPLY signs around town and almost all my aunts and uncles got first jobs in fancy hotels, working as busboys and maids ("shakin' sheets at the Drake" was the phrase).

My grandmother became the hostess at the Drake's brass-and-shellacked-halyard seafood restaurant. But she couldn't go to work through the Drake's swank, brassy lobby. She couldn't freshen up in the marble, golden-lit ladies' room, alongside women from Astor Place and Lake Forest. The help always had to come in through an unmarked door in the alley, and change in cold, concrete restrooms with dim bulbs.

So in the ICU I told my mother, "Saying, 'Never be afraid to go into a classy place, baby,' must have been a way to tell our daughter, 'Our family has paid its dues.'"

My mother raised the hand with an intravenous drip in it to say that I was exercising too much imagination.

"I just thought I might never get to show Elise a place like the

Art Institute. But what could she appreciate at her age? A really classy bathroom."

And a few minutes later, she opened her eyes long enough to add, "Show children the best people and places. Let them know they belong."

I love holding my mother's hand. Haven't held it like this since I was 9. Why did I stop? I thought it unmanly? What crap.

22

ICU seems to be staffed by good, smart young docs who think they know everything, and wise RN's who really do.

My mother's life was running out and I don't believe there was medical care to give her much more. But there was a difference between the care my mother got, hour to hour, from nurses and technicians, who were invariably considerate, gentle, and self-less, and that of most of her doctors, who were . . . invisible. Young, new doctors, who had just begun their residencies that month, would look in on my mother, check readings, ask a few questions, and defer all she had in return to her regular doctors, who they said were in charge of her care.

My mother's internist never saw her in the hospital (though he charged an extra fee for his patients to receive top-shelf ser-vice; I abhor that on principle, but not in practice for my mother). He sent me a few text messages before I arrived ("Scott, your mom is about the same . . ."), and one ten days after she died ("I just returned from being away. I went to check on your mom to find she passed away . . ."), which, by the time we received it, could only make us laugh.

My mother's pulmonologist had signed her into the hospital. But she didn't see her thereafter.

There were senior physicians who seemed to supervise the new young residents; I saw them huddled over laptop screens in the hallway, pointing to something with the tips of their pens. But I recall only two ranking doctors who walked the few paces into the room to actually meet the patient, listen to her breathing, look into my mother's eyes, take her hand, and hear her voice.

Maybe someday all medical care will be this way; I'm sure that it offers many efficiencies. But in the hospital, it felt remote, cold, and uncaring.

That morning a clutch of residents around my mother's bed explained that using a medication to try to shrink whatever bloomed in her lung risked bleeding in her stomach. They said they'd call my mother's pulmonologist to decide.

"Well, lots of luck," I told them. "She never returns my calls." The chief young resident offered a small smile and said, "We have our ways."

By the time I had descended to the cafeteria, my phone trilled.

"I hear you've been denouncing me on the floor!"

Of course I knew it was the pulmonologist. I could see the name on my phone; I felt the sting of her opening volley. But I drew out a pause, as if trying to place a name, before I replied, "I'm sorry, I don't recognize your voice. Can you tell me who this is?"

I sat down to hear the pulmonologist sputter. I wondered what medical protocol advised a doctor to yell at the son of a critically ill patient, but I was eager to make peace, for my mother's sake.

"I'm sorry we had to meet this way," I ventured after a few

minutes, and the doctor finally ran out of outrage. She assured me that she had daily phone conversations with the residents, and could follow my mother's vital signs with each bleep and blat.

"I wish we had some answers in your mother's case," she said. "She's such a lovely woman. But we just don't."

There were people in front of me who fretted over what they wanted in their burrito. "Black beans, please. And how hot is that green sauce?" There were people ordering 7Up and pulling up their socks, and children drawing smiles in puffs of steam they had blown onto the glass in front of the food. I thought of the Auden poem about how death takes place:

While someone else is eating or opening a window or just walking dully along.

"I understand," I told the doctor. "I know you're busy. But do you think you could find a few minutes to tell that to my mother? You know her. She trusts you. It would be what she needs to hear to understand, and our family would be grateful."

I heard what sounded like a puff of exasperation from the pulmonologist. No doubt she was busy. My mother told me she had two young children. But she said, "Later, maybe. I'll try to come by before I leave tonight."

I got into a food line, but was too fidgety to wait and too anxious to eat. I came back to my mother's room. Her eyes were closed, but she heard me.

"Baby."

She lifted her eyes slowly and I reached for her hand.

"I talked to Dr. Shure," I told her.

"Yes."

"And she says you're a lovely person."

"Well, how lovely of her to say that."

I drew up a chair and squeezed my hand a little more around my mother's.

"She also says, 'I wish we had some answers in your mother's case. We just don't.'"

My mother's response was quick and calm. There were beeps and bleats from the machines, but her voice was strong, clear, and unhurried.

"Oh, I knew that, baby. That's why no one wants to talk to me."

I sat for a long moment with my mother's hand in mine, then knelt down to kiss the back of her hand. I rubbed her wrist and kissed the top of her fingers, which seemed the best way to say the only thing I could think to: that I loved her, that she had given everything she was to me, and that I was here to give her all of what was left within me now. I lifted my head to tell her, "And Dr. Shure says she'll try to come by to see you tonight, before she leaves."

My mother lifted her eyes and mouth to smile.

"It's a whole four floors away," she said. "I won't hold my breath."

I sat on the edge of my mother's bed and once again jiggled the oxygen tubes in her nose. I dabbed the drops with a finger before they could drop to her lips.

"Besides," she said, "we have better things to talk about, don't we?"

When my mother woke briefly I sang her My Best Girl. She replied w/ You Are the Sunshine of My Life. Broadway in the ICU.

23

Wish clever minds that invented the Space Shuttle or Roomba could devise an oxygen mask that doesn't slip every 20 mins.

"You gave such great parties," I told her.

"Oh, we had some fun, didn't we, baby?"

My mother loved to entertain. Big parties were impossible in our one-bedroom box, but my mother loved to bring five or six people around our small round table and set out white plates, a silver-plated water pitcher, and tall turquoise water goblets, which lent refinement to whatever she served (her chili—cinnamon was the secret ingredient—over cornbread flecked with green pepper was in high demand).

She entertained friends to thank them for trudging through snow to see me in a school play, or to console a friend who had lost her job or her boyfriend (or had quit her job or boyfriend). She loved to gather a group in front of the TV to eat takeout chow mein and watch a world crisis, *The Wizard of Oz,* the World Series, or the Miss America Pageant.

She also brought up card tables from our storage locker to seat a dozen people for Christmas-Hanukkah dinners (the holidays were fused together in our mixed-faith family), plunking menorahs atop the table among the little Virgin Mary votive lights she'd find at Mexican markets.

Now and then a guest would admonish my mother, "You know, votive lights and menorahs aren't candlesticks. They're, you know, religious things."

"But don't they make things prettier?" my mother would reply. "Isn't that what the holidays are all about?"

Two or three of my aunties, among Abba, Chris, Elaine, Geri, Marion, and Melba, were usually at the table, and a circle of people who were important to us. There was Uncle Waltie, my Aunt Chris's off-and-on boyfriend (they would marry for a few years, after about twenty-five of breaking up and getting back together), who talked like a red-blooded socialist but worked in personnel at a blue-chip bank. Chris, a committed Republican, would wave a stick in his face.

"I wouldn't want to spend a weekend in Niagara Falls with Richard Nixon," she'd say. "But isn't he smart?"

Uncle Waltie would fulminate.

"Balls, Chrissy. *Balls*. Someday, the people will rise up and take back this country!"

"They did, dearie," she'd tell him. "And elected Nixon!"

"Balls!"

"Boobies!"

"Balls!"

(I now recognize this as foreplay.)

They often brought along Clem, a charming, elderly neighbor with a red Christmas-plum-pudding nose, who kept a cigarette and a scotch within reach, and told me stories about his boyhood on a Missouri farm that starred, no doubt to amuse me, tumescent bulls and stallions. There was Jim, an ad man, for whom my mother mixed one martini after another, which left a pile of tiny plastic swords from his cocktail onions under his elbow; by the time my mother brought out dessert, Jim's spot at the table looked like the aftermath of the Battle of Agincourt between toy soldiers. And there was Uncle Gene, who puffed a pipe, designed department store windows, and would walk into our apartment for Christmas-Hanukkah dinners wailing, "I'm positively up to my *ay-asss* in *elllves!*"

Auntie Marion and Uncle Charlie Grimm came to a lot of holiday dinners after they were married. Charlie was often asked to carve the entrée, and his old first-baseman hands, huge as hams and studded with scars, would be nimble and delicate (Charlie was the first man I knew whose hands were always glossy from a fresh manicure).

He'd hold the knife above a bird or roast and say, "This reminds me of a gal I knew in Pawtucket . . . ," and folks at the table would howl back, "Char-lee!"

He'd smile down at me, his face leathery from so many day games at Wrigley Field.

"Awww, c'mon. Let the kid hear a little poetry."

My mother always invited my father to those holiday dinners. I understand now the character that took for both of them. She didn't want him to be alone. She didn't want me to be without my father.

In the hospital now my mother asked, "Do you remember Dad and the electric carving knife?"

"Yeeow!"

It was a newfangled invention of the age in the time of power steering and coffee percolators. *Man harnesses electricity to carve . . . bologna! Imagine!*

We gathered round this enchanted implement the way early man first beheld fire. We oohed and aahed to slice through a loaf of bread, a roll of toilet tissue, and that day's *Chicago Daily News*.

Then my father began to imagine how biblical history might be different had ancient mohels used such a knife for circumcisions.

"Oy vey, sorry, Abraham!" he said, his ancient mohel hands rattling. "Guess no Little Abes now!"

"Do you remember what you said?"

My mother crinkled her nose.

"Kind of . . ."

"You waited until all the laughs he got gave out, then said, 'Ernest's religious heritage is so important to him, isn't it?'"

My mother laughed now, but mostly at my imitation of her wide-eyed comic delivery.

"Do you remember the night we saw some gal in the building across the way through the window?"

"Shimmy into her girdle?" my mother asked.

"I saw her a couple years later, you know. In a snowstorm, we shared a cab. She said, 'Oh, you look out on Division Street; that's where I live. Small world.' I wanted to say, 'You have no idea.'"

There were usually no other children when my mother entertained. After half an hour or so, the adults would give up on efforts to make child-centric conversation with me ("So, what are you studying in the fifth grade? South America? Like, Brazil and stuff, right? They've got an awful lot of coffee in Brazil . . ."), and I was glad. It was more fun to be a fly at their table, and to overhear their stories about work, romance, and the jokes with naughty punch lines that made them laugh deeply and roll in their seats.

My mother referred to many of these gatherings as "foundlings" parties. Gene, Jim, Blair, Leo—so many of my "uncles"—had come to Chicago from one of Sandburg's "little soft cities," outside of Chicago. They often seemed to remark, "I don't talk to my family," or, "I haven't seen my mother or father in years."

My inklings grew as I got older, until one morning I just asked: "Gene, Jim, and the rest—are they fruits?"

I cringe now to recall that I used to use the word. What is it that politicians say when caught by some old boorishness? "I was a man of my time and place." I was a thirteen-year-old kid, looking for a chance to be a little shocking.

My mother sat down with me at the kitchen table.

"Do you mean homosexuals?"

"Yeah. I guess," I told her.

"I guess I don't really know," she said. "Perhaps. So?"

She mentioned some of their hometowns—places like Rockford, Bettendorf, and St. Joseph—and said, "They moved to Chicago because they didn't fit into those small towns. People from all over the world find a place here. But their families may not understand the way they are. We're not their family. But we can give them a drink and a good meal and a place to laugh. We can care about them. You know, dear," she said, "if you really want to do something creative, you'll meet a lot of people like them."

"But how do they know about real life?" I asked. "When they're ... different."

I remember my mother taking a long pause and reaching over for my rye toast.

"Do you think they really are ... different?"

My mother matched my pause, and went on.

"They sure know about love. They know about loneliness. They know how to be funny. Maybe all creative people are a little different. Being a little bit of an outsider helps you see things other people may miss. That's why so many artists are outsiders, you know. One way or another."

I remember how my mother pushed back from the table. She was disappointed, irritated, and had to get ready for work.

"I think we're pretty lucky to know them," she called back from the hallway. "Don't you?"

My mother inched herself up slightly to ask, "Remember the James Bond party?"

"Everybody does," I told her. "I don't see a grade school pal who doesn't talk about it. As much as we sing 'Sunrise, Sunset.'"

I was about to turn thirteen. My mother and I would attend nineteen bar or bat mitzvahs of my schoolmates that year (which etches the lyrics of "Sunrise, Sunset" into you for life). None of my friends had bar or bat mitzvah safaris, balloon rides, or any other festivities to merit a *New Yorker* cartoon. But their parents gave some splendid parties, with buffet tables, ice-cream cakes, and bands.

My own religious convictions were mixed to skeptical, pulled between Catholicism, Judaism, and agnosticism. I didn't want a bar mitzvah. But I was not a skeptic about parties. My mother wanted to throw one that would not make me feel shortchanged for standing by our family's mixed beliefs.

So if I could not become a man at the age of thirteen, as in a bar mitzvah, I could be a spy. My mother gave me a James Bond party.

And not just a party with little plastic spy badges. My mother wrote the invitations in lemon juice, on royal blue airmail paper, then sent the envelopes in a pouch to the London office of her ad agency. A Londoner named Maggie, a secretary like my mother, thought the idea was charming, stamped the envelopes, and sent them back to Chicago, where my pals thrilled to see Royal Mail postmarks and stamps bearing the queen's profile. The blank-looking thin blue page had a note to instruct the recipient to hold it carefully above a candle: the invitation to my birthday party would be revealed (which is probably not how Her Majesty's Secret Service passes messages to its field agents).

It was a birthday party and *scavenger hunt* that sent my pals into the streets of the Loop. My mother, aunties, and uncles concocted clues like, "Follow the river to Michigan until you see the Great Wall of China," which was a clue to walk along the Chicago River to the Michigan Avenue bridge and the *Chicago Tribune* building, which, as most Chicago school kids know, is faced with stones from the Great Wall of China and almost 140 other buildings. They followed a trail to aunties and uncles, positioned at strategic civic monuments, to receive the next clue, and on and on to the final "treasure," which I cannot recall.

Twelve- and thirteen-year-olds chasing clues through the hurly-burly of Chicago's Loop is an unimaginable motif for a kid's birthday party these days. But the scavenger hunt challenged and enthralled us.

"You all had fun, didn't you?" my mother asked now. "I know we did."

"Running and laughing through the Loop—scratching our heads, trying to figure out stuff—we loved it," I told her. "It gave us a glimpse of being grown up. As much as a bar mitzvah," I told her.

My mother gave dinners that happily coincided with some of my classroom projects. When I had to make a topographically correct map of North America out of flour, water, and food dye, it was Gene, the display-window designer, who whipped up the

Rockies and died them purple, glazed the peaks with sugar, and topped off Pikes Peak with a pipe-cleaner climber.

"Yo-del-ay-ee-hoo!" he puffed over his pipe and scotch. "Yo-del-ay-ee-hoo!"

When I had to dress as King Hussein for a grade-school class, it was Auntie Chris, who had sewn her own ensemble in her dancing days, who stitched a burnoose out of a swatch of nubby upholstery cloth on which I had sketched a camel. My burnoose was about as true to Hashemite tribal garb as a little green leprechaun's derby is to an Irishman. But I got an incongruously good grade for Auntie Chris's sewing.

Auntie Melba was at the table the night I worked over the single-sheet newspaper I put out in the seventh grade. In a sense, she was the publisher: *The Seventh Grade Express* would not have appeared if Melba and my mother hadn't run twenty-five sheets through the office copier at the ad agency.

"But we've only got twenty kids in the class," I told them.

"You always save a few for awards committees," said Melba.

I wanted to be a writer and had read just enough to sound preposterous (*The sixth-grade kickball team, rousing itself from the stark specter of inglorious defeat like Spartans at Thermopylae . . .*). Melba would lower her glasses on her nose to try to follow one of my sentences, as if she were trying to locate the Via Cavour on a street map of Rome. Then she'd look up.

"Do you just want people to know you've done your homework," she'd ask, "or to actually read this?" I still try to ask myself that question.

As I grew older, my mother's principles of hospitality (which were really principles of life) sometimes opened silly little differences between us. She set a beautiful table: solid white plates, crisp white napkins, and pale blue place mats, which conveyed a sense of harmony and order (I see now that these were theater skills). Then she spiced the table with a sprinkling of cute little thingies (painted wooden napkin rings that looked like fish, a creamer that looked like a cow that we called Mrs. O'Leary's Creamer) from crates and barrels of the original Crate and Barrel store, which was in an old elevator factory on Wells Street.

My mother believed a peaceful table put people at ease. But I rejected uniformity in all its forms. For years after I got out on my own, I made a point of having nothing in my kitchen that matched. I'd get a plate here, a plate there, and coffee mugs from souvenir stands, craft shops, junk shops, political campaigns (and, in time, an awful lot of public radio stations). Anyone who opened my kitchen cabinet could tell I had been to El Salvador, cheered for the Cubs, changed planes in Miami, and that Marion Kennedy Volini was my alderman.

"Such chaos!" my mother used to exclaim. "It must make people nervous just to sit there. The whole idea of entertaining—even if it's just a couple people—is to talk. The table should be calm and orderly."

My mother had place cards at the table for as few as four guests. As a child, it was my job to write out names on the cards, and draw aptly cute artwork (flowers, trees, astronauts) to fit.

(I have never received such unstinted praise as that which my mother's friends bestowed for writing their names in a juvenile scrawl.)

"Place cards make people comfortable," my mother used to say. "So they know you've been waiting for them. You've made a place just for them. They don't have to ask, 'Uh, where do I go?' They can see you're not just saying, 'Oh, find a seat somewhere down there.'"

As I got older, I questioned the need for place cards. I thought it smacked of regimentation, authoritarianism, and privilege (which, clearly, I had only seen in movies). Yet aside from a few small japes, I'd indulge my mother, and continued to write out the names, expanding my artwork into indistinct thumbnail caricatures of the guests.

But in high school, I was elected president of the statewide student council. My mother decided to throw a small party to thank some friends who had helped me. It was a lovely idea. She planned a thoughtful menu (hamburgers and hot dogs, but with Dijon mustard and poppy seed buns, and baked potatoes with a posh sprinkling of chives). She baked cookies that we decorated as campaign buttons. She set out the small vigil candles that she loved.

I looked down at the table just before guests would begin to arrive, and I was appalled. My mother had put out place cards.

"Place cards!" I fumed. "The table belongs to the people! The people should be able to sit where the people want!" I might have sung a few lines from a Leonard Cohen song. "There's a revolution going on!" I sputtered. "'There's something happenin' here; what it is ain't exactly clear,!" Then I got to my true teenage worry. *"Don't embarrass me with place cards!"*

My mother said nothing but turned softly and I could see (she didn't do this often) that she was crying.

"I'm sorry. I just try to treat your friends graciously. But I know the world is changing, young people have different ideas. I don't want to embarrass you. . . ."

My arms were around her as I babbled apologies before she could pull the first place card.

Then our apartment buzzer began to ring. A couple of friends named George and Alfred arrived. They wore black berets and turtleneck shirts in admiration and emulation of the Black Panthers. As they approached the table, I braced myself for fiery,

Cleaveresque denunciations of decadence, materialism, and the tyranny of place cards. George squinted slightly as he bent down to read the names above the plates.

"You're over here, Alfred," he said. "Do you see me over there?"

"You were right about place cards," I told her in the hospital now. "Remember George?"

"The Black Panther?"

"I think he's a banker now."

"Yes. Darling young man."

"He loved your place cards. He could see your graciousness. I was letting a lot of adolescent pomposity get in the way."

"Do you and Caroline use place cards?"

"For breakfast," I assured her.

A bolt of pain stabbed my mother. I saw it explode behind her eyes and roll around her head. I clenched her hand, then her arm, as she bucked slightly and trembled a lot and seemed to try to kick herself out of the bed in which she felt some sharp, dirty dagger was being twisted in her chest.

I held on to her arm. My mother gasped for a last breath and fell back on the pillow.

Then she breathed again.

I blotted moisture from her mouth with the back of my hand. I repositioned the oxygen tubes in her nose, found it hard to reach over for a tissue, so I ran a finger to flick off the drops that were beginning to clog her nose.

"This is so . . . I'm so . . . ashamed," she said, and I shushed my mother the way I remembered her running a hand over my head to tell me I could feel safe, I could close my eyes, I could stop thinking and fall asleep.

"Shuuush," I said. "I'm here."

"I can't take many more of those."

"No. No. No . . ." And by then quick, firm steps had brought a nurse to the door and my mother had sunk into sleep, or at least closed her eyes. Mary came forward to flick some lights and buzzers but then turned away on soft feet and gently rolled the door closed behind us.

Half an hour later, my mother opened her eyes and blinked.

"The name cards. The kids make them?"

"Yes. Animals, pirates. A different color for each name."

"It's good to get them involved."

"They pass out olives and nuts. They love to check coats. They've got an elaborate system, with numbers and tickets."

My mother smiled.

"Does everyone get their coat?"

"There're some hits and misses," I told her. "You know the greatest entertaining you ever did?"

My mother tilted her head.

"Lar 'America First' Daly."

"The man in the Uncle Sam suit?"

Between aldermanic, congressional, senatorial, and presidential elections, Lar "America First" Daly was on a ballot every few months. He was a tall man with white hair and a rich voice who indeed campaigned in an Uncle Sam suit. This alone earned him a photo in the newspaper every few years.

Lar Daly was often compared to Harold Stassen for electoral futility. But Harold Stassen had been a governor, a naval commander, and had signed the United Nations charter. Lar Daly had never been elected dogcatcher. Now and then, his vote totals would amount to a few digits, perhaps because his last name was just a vowel short of Chicago's mayor's.

Lar Daly was really a champion litigant. He successfully sued to have "America First" included in his name on the ballot, and won a ruling from the FCC in 1960 that forced NBC to put him on the Jack Paar show for forty-seven minutes, equal time to what Richard Nixon and John F. Kennedy had received.

Years later, Lar Daly was running (again) for mayor of Chicago. I was running an underground student newspaper, and we officiously invited all candidates on the ballot to be interviewed by our editorial board. We got no response from Mayor Daley or his doomed Republican opponent, and none from the Communists, the Socialist Workers, the Peace and Freedom Party, the American Independent Party, or even the publicity-famished Vegetarians.

Lar Daly wrote back. He said he'd come to our office (which of course was the one-bedroom apartment I shared with my mother on the North Side).

I got a couple of pals to be the editorial board, which could not meet with Candidate Daly until after the editorial board had gotten out of algebra.

My mother laid out corn chips and peanut butter sandwiches. Our buzzer rang promptly at the appointed time. Lar Daly wore a worn old gray suit with elephant-ear lapels for our meeting, but doffed his towering Uncle Sam hat to my mother when she opened the door.

"Ah, it sure is nice to enter hostile territory," he said, "and see a pretty face."

I forget what urgent questions we asked Lar Daly. He said a few crackpot things I can't recall, and several that made our editorial board of sardonic youngsters roll our eyes— "Public schools are a mess," and "The U.S. government snoops on everybody"—things that make me wonder today why we sneered.

Lar Daly brightened when my mother asked about his Uncle Sam hat.

"You just don't buy that in a costume shop, do you?" she asked. "I can tell from here—the stitching is just exquisite."

"Good eye, ma'am. I got a Lithuanian woman who works for me, sews it all by hand. I'll go through two or three of these a year. You see, I keep stuff here"—he shook out papers at the bottom of his hat—"kinda like my office, so I can keep both hands free to meet people. Lincoln kept his office in his hat, too, when he was a young buck prairie lawyer. People laughed at him in those days, too. Trying to be a lawyer with no education, that squeaky voice, and those long legs growing out of his suits."

Our editorial board had been in session for more than an hour, and Lar Daly (who did not leave an impression that invited further comparisons to Lincoln) picked up his hat and began his good-byes.

"I know you must have a campaign appearance to make," my mother told him. "But please don't run off until we've at least given you a drink for your trouble."

He did have one (scotch, rocks, as I recall), and then one more for the road. My mother brought out peanuts, and some kind of cheese with little toasts.

"You know, I run a bar stool company," he told us. "Business is okay. But the glory days was back when I was young, in the thirties. Bookies needed stools. You know why, Mrs. Simon?"

My mother leaned forward. "I was a child."

"They couldn't sit at desks and post the numbers on a blackboard. So they sat and stood on stools. The cops knew where all the betting parlors were, 'cause they'd bust 'em. I'd tell the cops, 'Give me an address, and you'll get fifty cents for each stool we sell.' The cops would raid them every few weeks, remove the furniture, and the books would just reopen and buy more stools. It kept business flowing, lemme tell you."

The second scotch and the reminiscence seemed to make Lar Daly's eyes a little watery.

"But I guess the glory days are always when we're young. Right, Mrs. Simon?"

"You are so right, Mr. Daly," she told him.

"I got six kids," he said between sips. "All grown now. I know people make jokes about me, and I always worried about them getting hurt. 'Hey, is your dad that crazy guy in the Uncle Sam suit?' Kids can be jerks. But I'd tell my kids—and Mrs. Simon, I'll tell your boy here—hey, you can't let a little razzing get you down. You gotta do what you believe in. Hey, they all laughed at Christopher Columbus, didn't they? But he brought home the gold, didn't he?"

"You were the soul of graciousness that day," I told my mother now. "With a man most people would have laughed down the stairs."

"He was a guest in our home," she said. "I'm not sure I'd want him to be president. Or even dogcatcher. But he sure dedicated his life, didn't he?"

"You saw that," I told her. "I was trying to be sophisticated and cynical—like a journalist in the movies—and just saw the crackpot. You were gracious, and found the human being. I hope I remember that now."

"Oh, you always do that when you talk to people, baby."

"I meant in life. You know," I said as a memory snapped into place, "I remember, weeks later, reading the vote totals in the paper. Lar 'America First' Daly got something like six votes in our ward, didn't he? I said to you, 'That must be people who think he was the mayor.'"

The moment came into my mother's memory, too.

"And I told you, 'That's not why *I* voted for him.'"

We drew ourselves back into the cloud of laughter we had shared so many years before.

"Well, the poor man drove up all the way from the South Side," my mother said. "Just to talk to a high school kid. You made him feel like a real candidate, and he let you feel like a real reporter. That earned my vote."

"The entertaining you did," I told her. "I figured out a few years ago why."

"Why not? It was fun."

"It was just you and me. Dad wasn't around, or dependable. But you enlarged our circle. You gave a kind of home to all of the aunties and the uncles. They taught me stuff and enriched our lives."

"You gave them something too, baby," my mother told me. "It's hard to be alone like they were. Maybe some of that's changing."

"Do you remember Hy's little joke?" I asked her.

"He had so many."

"This one was really *r-r-r-aw*. . . . "

"Oh, that!"

Hy, the boxer who became the bra man, was a guest one night when my mother had six or eight people at the table and on the couch, and talk turned to a story in the paper about an assistant coach on the Chicago Bears who had such an unruly appetite he'd run out of the team's training camp in rural Indiana to eat raw ears of corn.

"*R-r-r-aw*," said Auntie Chris with contempt. "Utterly *r-r-r-aw*, can you imagine? And he's not some poor migrant worker, but a fat, well-fed coach. How can he discipline young men? *R-r-r-aw*," she repeated. "Utterly *r-r-r-aw*."

After a lot of *yucks* and *eeews* around the table, Hy piped up.

"All that corn silk," he said. "He probably just thought he was eating a blonde."

The living room roared and rocked with laughter. I felt my face flush as people looked to see if I understood what Hy had said. I was about twelve and didn't. But to try to look wise I joined the laughing until all my aunties and uncles began to lean across the table to kiss my forehead and rustle my hair. I realized, in the wash of loving laughter that followed a foul, funny joke I didn't understand, that my mother had made a pretty sweet place for me in the world.

Thank you for all yr warm wishes and prayers. Such love drives the world.

24

Thought that my mother won't get another glimpse of the city she loves is unbearable. My wife, from France, points out—

"She is seeing Chicago in the faces of the loving, tough, & kind souls working so hard for her in the ICU."

My phone trilled as the squeak of carts announced rounds. It was a friend who is my doctor at the Cleveland Clinic. I have a spinal condition that was growing worse (which I hid from my mother in the hospital; I would get surgery three months after she died). He knew and liked my mother, and when I told him what I knew he said, "Well, of course radiation treatment can deteriorate the lungs."

Despite the time difference, I phoned my wife.

"Why are we just hearing this?"

The doctor who had overseen my mother's radiation treatment was a short, solid physician of distinction who talked a lot about herself and the patients she'd treated who were household names.

I wouldn't be surprised to hear that she's talking about my mother now. Just to raise my mother's stock with the doctor, I had wildly exaggerated how well we knew some of those names too.

The doctor called herself *blunt* as tirelessly as a used car salesman calls himself *honest*. "You're just too old and rickety for surgery, darling," she had told my mother when they first spied new cancer in her lungs. I thought how much nicer it would sound to call an eighty-four-year-old woman by her name. "Excuse me, but I'm blunt," she'd usually add. "Some people can't handle that."

I told my wife I thought the doctor was putting on an elaborate act. "She's like Kathy Bates playing a cancer specialist," I told Caroline. "The way I played James Bond when I was twelve." But if the doctor's act could help my mother, I'd clap along.

The doctor told us the dosage of radiation would build with each treatment. I flew out to join my mother, whose sessions would finish by midmorning. We'd stop for breakfast thereafter. ("Look around," she'd tell me. "Who has breakfast at ten thirty in the morning? People who've had a helluva night and are just getting up. And radiation patients who've had a helluva morning.") Her spirits and humor—and her appetite—had been strong.

But after an hour or so my mother would put down her fork and announce, "I'm sorry. I've just got to go home," and then she'd sleep through the day.

Well, she was in her eighties. She'd gotten up early, couldn't eat or drink, had taken a tranquilizer, and had spent forty-five minutes tied up like a hostage, being zapped with a ray strong enough to peel paint. I'd kiss my mother on the forehead and leave (then fall asleep on the plane).

But my mother's husband told us how each radiation session seemed to leave my mother a little weaker for a little longer; and then weaker for longer yet. Her last nine sessions were spaced over just two weeks. We wondered if doctors were trying to complete the course before the holidays.

I sent a note of concern to the doctor and got this response after a few days (caps hers): "REST ASSURED WE ARE TAKING EXCELLENT CARE OF HER; THE SBRT TEAM IS A UNIQUELY TALENTED GROUP OF PROFESSIONALS, AND I WOULD LET THEM TREAT ME IF THE NEED AROSE (WHICH I HOPE IT DOES NOT)."

Of course it wasn't the care of the SBRT team we were worried about, but the doctor's. And I still don't know what SBRT means. Except perhaps, "If you have to ask, you don't know as much as we do."

The doctor proclaimed my mother "cancer-free" within a few months of her treatments. But she had never explained that the radiation therapy itself might weaken my mother's lungs.

And I don't know that it would have made a difference. I think I would have told my mother, "You're strong. You have grandchildren. Take radiation—please!" I think she would have done that for us.

But by that time, my mother had buried scores of friends. She was clear-eyed about her own perishability. And she deserved the information to make her own decision, even (or especially) the chance to say, "If it could weaken my lungs, I'll just take my chances, thank you." Unchecked, cancer might have just proceeded along at the same pace.

Doctors shouldn't cajole older people, like children. In the end, my mother, who so cherished a classic joke, died in a way that embodied one: she was that lady for whom the treatment was a success, but the patient died.

I was in my mother's room when the chorus of residents came by. The day before, they had asked if they could use a drug that might help her breathing but risked setting off bleeding in her intestinal tract. I phoned my doctor in Cleveland, who thought it was worth the chance, so we gave our agreement.

And now, twelve hours later, I asked how the drug was working.

"We're still waiting for it to come up from the pharmacy," a resident explained. "It's in the basement," she added, in a tone that made the basement sound like Ulaanbaatar.

"They have elevators in this city that go up a hundred floors. Why not up here to the ninth?"

I saw the residents pass glances in a circle around me, and got a small sense of what it might be like to be an elderly patient while young doctors talk around you.

"The pharmacist just hasn't sent it up," one of them finally replied.

"I'll go get it."

"They must be busy."

"That's why they're in business, isn't it? I didn't think my mother had a lot of time to waste. I could have flown to have it filled in New York—or Paris—and be back by now."

More silent glances.

"I don't know why everyone is so reluctant to talk to the pharmacist," I said with growing agitation. "I talk to powerful people for a living. Should I go down there?"

I know this last remark was smug. But ten minutes later, the medication arrived (and, to be fair to both residents and pharmacist, turned out to be useless).

A nurse popped it open to shoot it into the tube in my mother's chest while a couple of the residents looked away from me.

"Doctors," I told them, "I hope someday you have a son or daughter who will fight for you the way I will fight for my mother."

My mother opened her eyes and saw me perched at the end of the bed, trying to read a few paragraphs in the newspaper.

"When did I get old?" she asked.

"I never thought you have."

"Oh, pishposh. No, really. When?"

"I don't know." I tried out a number. "Seventy-five? No, later—eighty."

"I don't like old age."

"You don't look old," I told her. "Everybody tells you that."

"You ought to be inside this body," she said. "I guess I feel old just in time, don't I? It would be a shame for this to happen to someone who feels young. . . ."

My mother hated old age. She didn't like to walk slowly because her joints had turned both brittle and squishy, and she hated to hear people, even when (especially when) they meant to be nice, reassure her, "Oh, don't worry, no rush."

She didn't like to have to ask people to speak up. She didn't like to have to knock the edge of every jar of spaghetti sauce against the kitchen counter because her hands couldn't turn a lid.

She didn't like her hair getting thin and wispy. She didn't like her teeth cracking or her eyes clouding and she especially didn't like going up a dress size. Old isn't what my mother looked like in the mirror of her mind's eye.

She didn't like being dismissed as adorable or cute by younger people, as if she were a five-year-old, when she said she didn't understand a technological term or a dirty joke.

"Kids need you for everything," my mother told me. "Then they become young adults and think you know nothing."

My mother told me she wanted to get out of the hospital if only to march into a store nearby and return the phone we had gotten her.

"I know it can give you e-mail and photos and games and search civilization for you. But I want a *phone*. All the passwords it demands, like I'm a British spy."

We had brought her to that store; she'd taken some classes there. But all the bright young people in GENIUS shirts, whom my wife and I found delightful, faintly irritated my mother.

"Yes, they're all very smart," she said. "But it's not like any of them invented the wheel."

My mother didn't like losing friends every year. She didn't like going to their funerals and seeing the number of faces she knew dwindle. She didn't like getting together with pals for lunch and seeing a circle of six faces tighten to four, and she didn't like getting together with four or five and having to talk about aches, pains, and things that happened when they were young.

"When the phone rings now," she once told me, "I wonder if I shouldn't save some time and just ask, 'Cancer, stroke, or heart attack?'"

My wife and I used to talk about bringing my mother to live near us someday, perhaps in an apartment on another floor of our building. She loved her grandchildren. She loved being their

Grand-mère, taking them to art museums, holiday tea at the Drake, and shopping for dolls.

But my mother did not want to be a Granny, living in a studio apartment and waiting for small hands to knock on her door after school.

A couple of years before she died, we took my mother on a cruise that made stops in Sicily, Italy, Croatia, and Greece. I was ostensibly part of the ship's entertainment. But my mother was the real show. Passengers wanted her at their table for dinner. Strangers stopped me in the hallways to tell me, "Your mother said the most amusing thing . . ." Dapper, elderly gentlemen (and some of them not at all that elderly) sought me out to ask, "So, your mom. Is she available?"

"She's married."

"That's not what I asked," one of them told me, pretty plainly, and when I reported this to my mother she just laughed at that, as she had for, I don't know, maybe seventy years.

In several ports of call, she'd ring our cabin just before tours departed to say she felt a little wan and wouldn't join us.

"You have a good time, baby," she'd tell us. "I'm just going to rest. I'll see you when you get back."

So we'd get back from the day in Malta or Livorno to run into passengers we scarcely knew who'd say, "Hey, I saw your mother getting off the ship to go exploring. Did she tell you?"

She did not.

"She's eighty-three years old!" I'd exclaim to my wife, pacing like the sitcom dad of a rambunctious teenager. "People don't speak Italian with subtitles here. She only knows how to say spaghetti, linguine, and pasta con vongole."

(A rank injustice to my mother, who knew the names of a dozen different pastas, Italian movie stars, painters, sculptors, and that Dino Paul Crocetti was Dean Martin's real name.)

I was just warming up.

"Where do you think the Mafia got started?" I asked my wife. "Italian port towns! In Chicago, we know that! Why doesn't she just let us know where she is?"

Some passengers in the port of Livorno said they had seen my mother in the center of Pisa, half an hour away. Our ship pulled out in two hours. I imagined sobbing good-bye to my wife and daughters as the cruise ship set sail, then prowling Italian *tavernas* and *carceris* for my aging, miscreant mother.

"If this is what it's like to be parents of a teenager," I told my wife, "we're getting our daughters into a convent. Soon as possible!"

My wife and I left our daughters (instead) with friends on-board and were in line for a bus to Pisa to launch a last, frantic search for my mother with the Carabinieri when she clambered off a bus from Pisa. She looked radiant.

"I had the best lunch. Two glasses of wine. Bought some lovely cards. Actually never saw the tower, but met some lovely people and the lunch was sooo good. . . ."

In Malta she had another lunch and got a lift back to port from a man with a black Mercedes (we dubbed him the Last Knight of Malta). She also bought little Maltese cross necklaces for our daughters because she knew I wouldn't think of it (she was right).

I think that my mother loved being with us and she loved being on her own, footloose for just a few hours in a captivating, uncharted landscape where she could sit with a glass of wine and watch the world stroll by.

"Why didn't you call?" I asked her (and not softly).

"I was fine," she said. "Besides, how could I?"

We had removed the chip from her cell phone so my mother wouldn't get costly overseas calls from her beauty salon and people selling discount Florida vacations. There was no missing the firmness in her voice. If I was going to treat my mother like a teenager, she was proud to be a rebellious one.

The last night of the trip we congregated with some other passengers at midnight on the stern of the ship to write down wishes on small slips of paper. Then we tucked them into an empty champagne bottle to throw into the waves behind us.

"Your dad wanted to be a great father," my mother told me. The light of the moon made the snowy waves glow behind our boat as the small green drop of the bottle bounded along the top for a few skips, then disappeared.

"But things got in the way," she said. "You don't let things get in the way."

"Don't tell me what you wrote down in the bottle," I told her.

"I'll bet I don't have to," said my mother.

It was exhausting now just to breathe. Not just for her fragile lungs to take in breath, but for my mother to let it out and jiggle the tubes in her nose with every fifth or sixth gulp so the globs of water growing there didn't slide back into her nose or drip down into her mouth, all of which was disagreeable and humiliating.

I think my mother accepted that exhaustion and pain had to be part of the package. It was harder to bear how damn undignified dying could be.

"I don't think I'm smart or wise," she announced from under closed eyes.

"You are," I told her, and she brushed that aside with a sniffle.

"But I know more. I've seen more."

She blinked her eyes open.

"No one wants to listen to old people. I don't blame them. We can be so crabby. Things we know, that we see so clearly, and young people waste so much time finding out the same things all over again. But someone who's old and lonely has a lifetime to offer. We've gone to bed every night since our seventies thinking, 'Maybe I won't wake up.' That's why it's hard to sleep. That's why we're cranky and impatient. But we go to sleep anyway because we've learned what's really important in life. That's why people should talk to us."

There was a light rap of knuckles on the doorframe and a young voice called my mother's name from just behind the glass.

I am not sure my mother understands Twitter or why I tell her millions of people love her—but she says she's ver touched.

I think she wants me to pass along a couple of pieces of advice, ASAP. One: reach out to someone who seems lonely today.

And: listen to people in their 80's. They have looked across the street at death for a decade. They know what's vital.

25

I know end might be near as this is only day of my adulthood I've seen my mother and she hasn't asked, "Why that shirt?"

A couple of members of the palliative care team stepped into the room slowly. But this time my mother beamed, as if they were old friends from a past vacation.

"How are you, Doctors? So good to see you today. My son and I have been having the most wonderful time."

"Utterly, positively, absolutely true," I told them.

Dr. Ames, a young woman physician, came close to the bed, and my mother took her hand.

"And I am so grateful for everything you've done."

The last time these doctors had been at my mother's bedside, she had given them the heave-ho. She now offered gratitude in advance for any kindness for which she would not be around to thank them.

"That's why we came by," Dr. Benvolio, the other doctor, explained. "Is there anything else we can do for you?"

"Oh no," said my mother. "Things are just lovely. I'm here with my son. His wife and children—my grandchildren!—are on their way from California. We had the most wonderful visit with an old family friend, too."

"Father Chuck. Great guy. A Franciscan. *Priest,*" I added, if they hadn't quite understood.

"We were thinking maybe we can make things a little quieter," said Dr. Benvolio. "We can turn off some of the monitors in here. They'll still see how you're doing out at the desk," he quickly added. "But maybe you can get a little rest with less noise."

"Hear my jokes better," I suggested.

My mother smiled and took his hand, too.

"You've been so helpful. I'm so grateful."

I told my mother I would go downstairs for yet another cup of coffee, and slipped out with the doctors.

"Wow," said Dr. Benvolio. "She's really lovely." He shook his head with a little wonder. "She needs a lot of oxygen now. We're reaching the limits of what we can do, I think. What are your priorities?"

"My family is on their way," I told him.

Children weren't permitted on the intensive care unit.

"It's a crazy rule," Dr. Ames agreed. "But they wouldn't get past the guards downstairs. And maybe it's best anyway." She shrugged a shoulder in the direction of the lights, the beeps, and all the growling, grim alarms. "This is hard for kids to take in."

"So, being able to talk to the daughter-in-law," said Benvolio. "We'll work toward that."

The hours outside, ordered by the clock by which everyone else rose, ate, traveled, and worked, had begun to seem inconsequential here. We now lived and breathed on a planet of unrelenting yellow light and ghastly organ chords. I stared at my watch for a long moment when I looked at the time, as if I had to calculate for a time zone on the other side of the world.

"My family should land in four or five hours."

"And is there anything we can do for you?" he asked, in a soft, low tone. A kind of dream had been working in my mind: I wanted to take my mother for one last, long stroll down Michigan Avenue. I wanted her to look up into the skyline she had loved for so long, and into the store windows that she followed with the seasons. I imagined her waving to the lions in front of the Art Institute, and the tour boats, ore boats, and tugs plying the river below the Clark Street, State Street, and Michigan Avenue bridges.

But now I just asked, "Can I take my mother outside? Just across the street?"

The doctor flattened his lips.

"She needs a lot of oxygen."

"I'd just take her to the little park across the way," I told him. "We used to go there, just to sit and watch the city go by. Our daughters love to play there."

The doctors looked up at one another and when they didn't say no, I pressed on.

"I'll sign anything. Send security guards with me. Send the National Guard. Just please put my mother in a wheelchair, and let me bring her to the edge of the park. She'll feel the wind. She'll see her granddaughters at play and be surrounded by the city she loves. I am her *son*," I told them, and had to stop to find a breath. "I'll have my hands on her shoulders. I'll have my arms around her. If my mother dies on the spot—that very spot—we'll only be grateful."

The doctors looked at one another for a long moment before turning back to me.

"They have portable oxygen rigs," said Dr. Benvolio. "Let's see."

I went downstairs for coffee and when I returned, Anne had come on duty once more. She took me aside.

"Your mom says I get to meet your wife. And she's beautiful."

"Yes. Yes."

"Your mom is really looking forward to it," she said, "and wants to look her best. We'll help her. We'll get out her lipstick. We'll help with her hair. She says she feels like there's stuff between her teeth. She wants her favorite dental floss."

I paused.

"All these years, I've known that JFK was her favorite president and Nat King Cole was her favorite singer. I've missed her favorite dental floss."

"Maybe you'll recognize it at the drugstore."

"I'll be right back," I told her, and Anne dropped her voice enough so that I had to lean forward.

"And if you want to bring back a bottle of something," she said, "it'll look like plain old skim milk to me."

I could feel moisture in my eyes when I pulled back.

"South Side gals look out for each other," Anne said.

I came back to her room to find my mother with a pen in her hand and her hand quavering over a sheet of paper braced against a magazine.

"I have to write a note for Linda."

"You're in the hospital."

"A note with some cash. She made time for me"—Linda worked at beauty salons and barbershops nearby; she did my mother's nails every other week—"and then I never came."

"You're in the hospital," I reminded her.

"She needs this," she reminded me. "She has a little boy. I have to write Maria, too." She was a seamstress who had altered my mother's blue jeans when she recently lost an alarming amount of weight (some people would go to the doctor; my mother went to a seamstress).

The pen trembled in my mother's hand. She seemed to have been trying to write for some time and had managed to get only *D-e-a* down on paper, in shaky, tottering letters that might have startled someone who'd written beautifully composed cursive characters since she was a schoolgirl.

"I'll write it for you," I suggested.

"No one can read your writing."

She had me there. She struggled on.

"Oh nuts," she finally said, and let the pen drop onto her covers.

My mother was renowned for her notes, her thank-you notes especially (and in a way, even her condolence notes and letters to airlines, lawyers, doctors, and department stores wound up sounding like thank-you notes). Most were written by hand, in refined parochial schoolgirl script, using the edge of a laminated Infant of Prague mass card to compose her words along a straight line, then going back to add the tails of f's, p's, q's, and y's with a flourish. (I used to imagine Mr. Jefferson doing the same with a quill when he dashed, "*Life*, Liber*ty*, and the *p*ursuit o*f* Ha*pp*iness.")

My mother would prowl stores to find fine creamy papers (gray with black borders from the stationery racks at Marshall Field's when my father died), and the Art Institute shop for cards with Calder, Hopper, or de Kooning silk screens on the front. She'd write thank-you notes to those who invited her to dinner, to aldermen who left ice scrapers in her mailbox (and we didn't have a car), to priests for keeping departed friends in their prayers, and to the people who repaired her kitchen incinerator.

"I got a thank-you note from your mother," a Chicago banker told me. He and his wife had shared a cab with my mother and dropped her off after a play at a North Side theater. "It was so effusive—so elaborate—so beautifully written," he said, "you'd think we had given her a ride on the *Queen Mary*. And she enclosed a five-dollar bill for her share of the cab fare! Amazing!"

A talk show host told me she'd gotten a note from my mother, thanking her for mentioning me favorably on her program.

"It was adorable. It was delightful. I showed it to everyone," she said. "But I didn't write her back. I couldn't find good enough paper."

I wish we could find even twenty of those notes now. I've heard from many people who've said they'll always treasure a note that my mother wrote them. But I know: over the years they'd get folded away into forgotten places, used for bookmarks, coasters, and scratch pads. No one has misplaced more than I have.

A few people who had made it a point to keep one of her notes sent us copies after she died. We found a few more she had copied herself.

One is to a woman who was my mother's physical therapist after she had slipped on ice walking home from a cancer rehab treatment and cracked her cheek and collarbone:

Dear Edie

I found you to be a lovely person. You were patient and kind and did all you could to not only nurse my injury and aid me

*in the use of my arm but in addition you reinforced good
habits with my posture and giving me the necessary tools in
which to handle my body and live a more comfortable and
rewarding life. For all of this please know that I thank you.*

*... Please accept my sincere gratitude for all you did to
help me. I very much appreciate knowing you and appreciate
your professional ability. I am sincerely grateful to you. I feel
that we will meet again. Please know that I am thankful for
your presence in my therapy.*

*Warmly and sincerely,
Pat*

Then there was the note my mother wrote to the veterinarian who had seen her through several cats, and had to euthanize her last, the cranky, tubby, and pug-faced orange Ulysses:

Dear Dr. Dann:

*I truly appreciated all that you did to make it easier for Ulie
and also for me. The green towel that you so kindly provided
for his little body, the tranquilizing shot before the final
injection and your compassion through the entire travail.
I am so completely grateful to you. Doctor Dann, thank you
so very much.*

*The loss of these little creatures reaches a different depth of
our hearts, however, I am pleased in the knowledge that man
has been blessed with the companionship and comfort of
members of the animal kingdom and we are all better off for
having known and loved them.*

*I write this the night before the Thanksgiving holiday. It is
only fitting to tell you I am so grateful for having known you.*

*We do go back to about thirty years ago—once you were my
young friend and now I feel that you are my old friend. May
God keep you and those you love safe always.*

*Most sincerely
Pat*

There are so many more letters I wished I hadn't let drift
away. There were newsy notes my mother sent me every few
days at summer camp, typed after hours at the ad agency
where she worked, and filled with tales about friends and
family, movies she'd seen, where she'd gone, what she'd eaten,
and what she was certain I'd like when I got back. I'd give a
lot to be able to reread those now, and play them back in my
mind.

I don't remember throwing out any of my mother's letters. But
I'd read them over until the next arrived, so by the end of the
summer her notes would be folded and forgotten in magazines,
which I'd discard or leave behind, and paperback books, which
would get cast aside with each move.

Certainly my mother kept all of the notes I sent in return,
which I dashed off in maybe a minute (really, I put more effort
into writing the address on the envelope) on those couple of
nights a week we had to turn over a letter on our way into the
camp dining hall.

The notes from me to my mother are uninteresting, except
perhaps to see that I had handwriting like Charles Manson.

We've been able to find a few copies of letters that she had sent
my father after their divorce. I remember seeing some the night
he died, half a dozen notes bundled in a shoebox in the closet

of his hotel room, where I thought: He must have found them too painful to read, too precious to throw out.

I think my mother had banged out those notes on a typewriter, late at night, when the Loop had quieted and the El train would screech mournfully into turns. My father was jobless, broke, and trying to dry out (or not trying at all), bouncing between jobs and treatment programs in Miami, Cleveland, and Baltimore. I was sent to live with my aunt, uncle, and cousins in Washington, DC, while my mother worked several jobs in Chicago. My father had said and done some stupid, hurtful things. But my mother still addressed him with endearments. She signed off with chipper, cheering phrases, and expressions of a kind of love:

I must push my nose toward the stone that grinds.
    Loads and loads of all good and wonderful things, sweet boy:
    Luf—luf—luf

Patti

My mother seemed to fill her letters with the reassuring gossip of people who looked out for each other: who was working where, and who wasn't, who was drinking and who shouldn't, who was divorcing, and how the White Sox and Cubs were doing. Small, mundane details that told my father: we're apart, but a part of each of us will always know how to make the other laugh and smile. I'll bet it was often the only thought, at that time in his life, that gave him much joy.

A note written in February was addressed to us both. My father had found a gig at a club in Miami, and I joined him for a few weeks. He'd said he wasn't drinking, and had even taken up fishing. My visit was a reward for us both.

I remember eating sliced fried plantains, topped by crumbs of garlic and squiggles of cream sauce, in bright Cuban restaurants, and mornings that my father and I sat with gnarly men in saggy white shorts who set fishing poles in holsters along a dock and waited under the sun for the tip of their poles to jiggle by cracking open cans of beer. That turned out to be fishing.

We watched the evening news and saw snow pile up in Chicago (which seemed as far away as Siberia) and sent my mother a postcard with oranges or flamingos on the front, writing something like, "Went fishing today. How about you?"

She wrote us:

February 10
My dear Guys

The snow is up to your knees out there . . . by gar, was it fun getting to work today . . . WOW it took me an hour to get from the near north side, and this was on foot, by bus, by taxi, and by foot again.

Just checking in with you two joy boys as you bask in fairer climates . . . I'm jealous, as I have to wade thru ice, sleet, snow, and traffic tonight.

Just know, fellas, you ain't missing a thing in Chicago today!

Love and more love, to two beautiful
Brown-haired Valentines
Mow

(Mow, Dow, and Skow were family nicknames.)

I first read those notes when I was sixteen, as we packed up my father's clothes in his hotel room on the night he died. I tried to imagine how much they would have both delighted and wounded him. I saw the ways in which my mother tried to lend my father some of her strength, but as I read them now, as we pack her things, it stings me to see how much of her hurt I missed in those letters. Or did she keep those notes from me?

At one point she tells my father:

I am more lonely for my baby as each day goes by. It doesn't get better . . . it gets worse. At times I think there is within me some of the traits of my mother, I do get that despondent at times.

My father, after all, knew the secret of her mother's suicide, and could be trusted to keep it—for my sake. My mother didn't speak of it even when I was sixteen.

She sent him another note, apparently the morning after they had quarreled on the phone:

My dear Dow

So very sorry that you were in a blue-funk mood last night. I'm also sorry that when you started bringing up the ancient history of our divorce and such, that I "blew."

Ernie dear, as far as the reason for our divorce was concerned, please know that I bear no grudge . . . it was just a slice of life that happened . . . we all of us have our faults (heavens, you certainly know mine) and you should not be chided about it further . . . I must keep remembering, "Be there one among us without sin, let him cast the first stone" how true this is, your "fault" was just a "fault," a different kind of fault than mine perhaps . . . but nevertheless, just a fault. I could no longer accept the fault . . . that's all . . . so let

us not pursue this any further in our conversations . . .
PLEASE.

It may seem jarring in these times to see alcoholism referred to
as a fault instead of an illness. But my mother's view was mod-
ern in the 1960s, and reflected much of what we heard at Al-Anon
and Alcoholics Anonymous meetings (groups I respect perhaps
even more today).

Calling drinking a fault improved on calling it a sin. It gave
my father a chance to do something for himself—put down that
drink, for five minutes, five hours, then day by day—rather than
spend the only life he'd ever have sentenced to suffer an illness
with no known cure.

Seeing drinking as an illness can be too tidy. You don't catch
it, like pneumonia, or develop it, like a cancer. You have to take
a drink.

People who tell problem drinkers, "It's an illness; you can't
help it. Look at Churchill and Hemingway—they drank even
more," might score a point in a debate. But they do no favors
for their friends and loved ones. They give them nothing to go
on. My mother told my father that he had a fault. She also said
that she had her own, and placed them on the same scale. It was
a generous and loving view that set aside a thousand hurts and
slights.

She went on:

Had a very nice chat with Nelda [a friend] just before you
called, and we discussed the fact that at the present time I
feel so useless to my child, that he seems happier than he has
ever been, he is in a lovely home, has activity around him,
adores being among other children that I doubt he will ever,
ever be content to be with me again, even if I were married to

you . . . (what kind of life can we offer him now?). Nelda said
she could see much of what I was thinking but said, "Look,
when you call him, he's busy, and then he's excited . . . surely
there must be times, that when he lays his little head on his
pillow, he thinks of his Mommy and Daddy, and he wonders
where it will all end?" I think she may have a point, don't
you? . . .

I just drag myself from portal to portal. My mental
processes, nor attitudes have not been good . . . this feeling
sorry for myself is not good.

My very fondest, and sweetest thought to you dear one.

Be well, God keep you.
Patti

It hurts to read that letter today, and I want to cry out to my
mother, "Actually, when I laid my head on my pillow, I knew I
had two parents who loved me." I imagine my father reading that
same letter (I almost see the imprint of his fingers) over and over,
like a lovelorn teenager, looking for a loophole in each phrase.
He might have told himself, "If I could just change my fault, we
could be together again." But he couldn't.

In recent years there were e-mails my mother sent that have van-
ished along with fizzled hard drives, mail migrations, and mailbox cleanups. I recall a note my wife and I opened in China just
after our older daughter was put into our arms at an adoption
center. My quotation is approximate, but well remembered.

"Children connect you to eternity," she wrote us. "They're like
notes to be opened after we die."

My mother wrote notes to give thanks to people (and

sometimes the kinds of people who would stay nameless to many others). But she also wrote notes to remind herself how people had dotted her life with acts of grace, skill, and kindness. She wrote letters as a way to take stock of life.

I was with my mother a few years ago while I went over my day's e-mail. I paused occasionally to read her something that struck me as funny, outrageous, or sobering.

"Here's a sad one," I told her. The mother of someone who worked in a corporate department of our network had died. The department head announced condolences, funeral time, and passed on the best address for cards and flowers.

"You should write something right now," my mother told me. "Before you get on a plane and forget."

I didn't know the person who suffered the loss.

"I don't think I've ever met him. I don't think I've even seen his name until now."

"I'll bet he knows who you are."

"You don't think that he'd be puzzled to get a note from me?"

"I'll bet he'd find it thoughtful."

I fumbled for something to say, and just came up with silence.

"It'll take three minutes," she said. "Don't waste time trying to figure out how to avoid doing something good."

I wrote the note on the spot. And now, I try to write a note whenever I learn that someone in my circle of work or life, whether I really know them or not, has lost a parent or a spouse (or most wrenchingly, a child). I've written notes for bar and bat mitzvahs, birthdays, weddings, graduations, and funerals for people I don't know when someone reaches me to ask. I've never added up how much time it takes (I doubt it amounts to two hours a year), but several times a year I'm stopped by someone in an airport or on the street who says, "You don't know me, but you once sent a note. . . ." I'll walk off with a smile, and often a hug. It's a gift both from and for my mother.

Just spent 45 mins looking for mother' favorite dental floss. Waste of time? Act of faith.

Mother groans w/ pleasure—over flossing. "When they mention great little things in life, they usually forget flossing."

26

Breathing hard now. She sleeps, opens eyes a minute, sleeps. I sing, "I'll always be there, as frightened as you," to her.

My mother didn't sleep much now, but she closed her eyes between temperature-taking, bag-changing, sips of water and cups of ice, the way a passenger might close her eyes between stops on a long train ride. In the afternoon she lifted her eyes and announced, "I really need you to find Maria and Linda."

This was no longer her request or my promise. It was a last command. My mother knew that she was about to die. I was at her side; and her grandchildren and daughter-in-law were on their way. But my mother would not rest until she had settled a debt she felt she owed two women whom she cherished and admired.

I no longer scoffed at *rest* as a timid genteelism for *death*. I began to grasp that there comes a time when a person needs to die much as we need to sleep. My mother had reached that time. Death had become the only possibility of respite from suffering and fear. I wanted her to feel free just to lay back and rest: yes, to let go and die.

"Linda and Maria work so hard," my mother said, and took a long gasp. "They have children. Linda just showed me pictures of her six-year-old boy. So cute. They always make room for me and they rely on the cash. Go into my purse," she instructed me. "In the closet. Take out fifty dollars for each of them. Tell them thank you."

Her voice broke and her eyes hardened. She cleared her throat.

"Please. *Please*," she added softly.

"I'll tell them you'll see them soon."

Of course I didn't touch her purse. But I was glad to go on the errand, and a brisk walk through the busy streets my mother loved.

I scurried by big, bright store windows and thought of some of the young friends my mother had made on her strolls. "My friend Flora," she'd explain. "Loveliest young woman. From Serbia. Works at the Clinique [or Chanel, Hermès, or Lancôme] counter at Saks [or Macy's or Bloomingdale's]. I told her you were bringing the girls to visit and she said, 'Here, you must give them this.'"

(We still roll open drawers and find tiny foils of face cream or scented tissue my mother got from her friends and stuffed into our pockets for our daughters.)

The sun had started to graze the tops of the towers of the Loop and skipped great splashes of scarlet-gold light down the streets. I saw it as a kind of red carpet, unrolled to my mother's bedside.

I found Maria sitting under a throbbing white light behind her machine in the cleaning shop, a spray of pins in a ball of white thread at her elbow. She brightened.

"Your mom home?"

"I'm afraid not," I told her. "But she wanted you to have this."

I had some twenties folded into the hand that I held out to her. Maria didn't look and she didn't take my hand.

"I can't. Only when your mother can get her pants."

"She doesn't need them right now."

"When she does," Maria insisted.

"She wants you to have this now. Please. *Please*," I repeated. "Nothing would make her happier."

Maria took my hand and held it.

"I've been praying."

"That will make her happy, too."

"She's the greatest lady. The greatest."

I walked back into the street and thought how my mother had subverted an old saying: she was a hero to her tailor.

Linda worked at a barbershop above another tailor's shop in an old brown apartment building. When I opened the door, I could smell soap, hairspray, and lavender.

Linda was helping a man take his soapy head out of a bowl, smiled at me, and fixed a towel around the man's wet hair before coming over to me in the doorway.

"Mrs. Newman's son." She smiled. "I've seen you."

But when I reached out with my hand, she felt a crumple of paper—a manicurist would know that I wasn't slipping her lottery tickets—and stepped back.

"I can't take that."

"Please. My mother insisted. She sent me over from the hospital."

"I didn't do anything. She got sick."

"You made time for her," I told her. "You've been a wonderful friend."

"I want to wait until I see her again."

"She wants you to have this now." And when Linda held back I remembered why sending me her way had been so important to my mother.

"My mother says you have a little boy."

Linda nodded and smiled. "Yes. He's six. I show her pictures; she shows me pictures of your girls."

"Well, you know, my mother once had a six-year-old boy," I said. "And she sold clothes, and worked in nightclubs and offices, and did everything she could to give him the best life she could." I paused and tried to stand a little taller. "And here I am. And we both want you to have this."

I threaded my way back to the hospital through the streets my mother and I loved, filled with rush-hour foot traffic, the lemony gleam of store lights, the shrill song of police whistles, and people picking up their feet to rush to buses home, or bars and restaurants.

(And I stopped for a bottle of red and a bottle of white.)

My mother's eyes were closed when I got back to her room, and I leaned over gently. She stirred.

"Did you get it done?"

"They send their love."

"But you didn't get out my purse . . . ," she said, and let the thought trail off. She had spaghetti tubes running out of her, and enough painkillers to stun a horse, but my mother still didn't miss a trick, or at least any of mine. I held her hand until I thought she could just about rest.

My family called from the airport. "Hi, Grand-mère!" Friends took our daughters to dinner and I brought my wife up to the ICU.

My mother and my wife were both ravishing. My wife had

shaken off the pallor of a long trip from the other side of the country to stand by my mother's bed, hold her hand, and turn her kind, brown eyes and bright smile on her to tell stories of the times we had in California and how we felt that somehow she was with us all the time. My mother had rallied all of her will just to sit up in bed, her eyes alight with laughter, as she told wry, funny stories about being stuck and poked and feeling as if she'd grown a clown's red nose with the gurgling tubes pinching her nostrils.

My wife and my mother agreed: I talked too much about my daughters. I ate too fast and talked with my mouth full. I bought too many shirts on sale.

My mother sat up and beamed and conducted herself like the hostess at the head of the table of a lively dinner party. She said things she knew would prompt funny stories, and make the circle of people around her feel cherished. My mother worked the room. She wrapped us in enchantment and hilarity. She was dying and now gave us the breath of hope and laughter we all needed to get through it.

"This is my daughter-in-law, Caroline," she told Anne. "Isn't she just beautiful? Caroline, Anne is just so wonderful. She was telling me the most wonderful story...."

Anne brought in plastic cups and ice, and we opened the bottle of white. Toasts rang out: "To Pat! To Mamacita! To Grand-mère! Patricia Lyons Simon Newman Gelbin!"

My mother sipped her wine through a straw and looked so jolly, hardy, and vibrant I began to feel that maybe she would fool us all and live. But I knew that she had already gone past us. She had seen a door open ahead and begun to move, not drift, toward it. She wanted only enough time to say good-bye and take a curtain call.

Our friends sent photos of our children from the restaurant

nearby. They looked happy, over great, pale dunes of pasta, sopped with red sauce. But we had learned that parents have to think like a baseball manager who has to pull a pitcher before, not after, he throws a bad pitch. We had planned trips to the park and the zoo, and a visit to a cheesecake bakery, but all the while knowing that bad news was ahead for them. My wife needed to get back to our daughters.

"I will see you in the morning, Pat," she said, her face shining. "I love you so much."

"And I love you so much, my dear."

They held hands and I told my mother, "I'm going to see Caroline downstairs, then be back. Can I get you anything?"

"You don't have the kids," said my mother. "Stop for a quickie!"

My family has landed! ICU nurse works on mother's hair, using makeup mirror. Almost falls. Mother: "Don't let that break!"

27

**Was my mother saving this line? My family flies in.
My wife & I joke about me sleeping in the ICU ("All
the beeps! Can't—**

**—you med people keep it down?") Tell my mother
I'll see my wife downstairs, back in 10. Mother says,
"Have a quickie!"**

Those were just about my mother's last words. I took my wife to
the lobby (and we stopped—for coffee) so she could get back to
our children. By the time I got back to my mother her eyes were
closed and her breaths sounded slow, steely, and cold, as if she
had to pull each up on an iron chain.

Anne rolled the door open slowly and quietly.

"It's good to see her sleep."

"Yes."

"I think she saved a lot of strength to see your wife."

"She sure gave us a great show."

Anne leaned down closer and kept her voice level.

"Even if it looks like your mother doesn't hear things, she might."

She slipped down a sheet and helped me slide into bed next to my mother. I slipped an arm around her shoulder. I put my hand over hers. I told my mother, "I'm here."

Derek was at work on the floor and I climbed back onto my orange mat so that he could clap the huge, hissing mask over my mother's face. I sat and shivered a little in that day's shirt and my undershorts.

"If I'd known I was coming to this pajama party," I told him, "I would have brought some pj's. At least a robe and slippers."

"You should sleep," he told me.

"Any breath could be her last. I should be awake for that."

"Mothers love to see their children sleep," he reminded me. "If she looks down and sees you asleep, she will be happy."

I dozed a little. I was so weary from being awake for two days that worry would no longer keep me alert. Carts squealed into the room every hour or so; Anne and Derek, and then Rosemary and Mr. Washington, and a couple of people new to us came in, took readings, and smiled down at my mother and me. When I was awake, I'd wave, pull myself into a chair, and hold my mother's hand. I'd sing. I'd remember more jokes. I'd hold a tissue to my mother's nose and rejigger her tubing. At a little before midnight, I phoned my wife, just a few blocks away.

I was on a saw-toothed edge of sleep when I heard my mother speak. Her voice was frail and raspy but utterly clear.

"Help. Me."

I sprang from my mat. I took her hands. Her eyes were wide and I leaned in to look into them. They were calm, unblinking, and beautiful. I am sure my mother was there behind her eyes, but I'm not sure that she saw me.

I brought my face close. I held her face in my hands.

Once more my mother said, *"Help. Me."*

I didn't hear it as a plea for me to help her live—I think we both knew that was beyond any human power—but to help her take a running jump through the last wall of dread and pain to get to what was beyond. It was a plea for me to help her break down the wall she had promised to break through for me.

In that horrifying and exquisite moment, I held my mother as I have held my children. I tried to look without blinking into her bottomless brown eyes. I told her, "I'm here. Look at me. Give me everything. Every fear, every pain. Leave them with me. I'm your son."

Our eyes locked for a long time.

When she asked for my help last night, we locked eyes. She calmed down. A look of love that surpasses understanding.

I crept over to the table and put on music. A true gentleman and his daughter sang, and I stretched out next to my mother and tried to join along:

And forevermore, that's how you'll stay . . .

Listening to Nat & Natalie sing Unforgettable. Mother & I sang it just two nights ago. Coles have better voices for sure.

Her passing might come any moment, or in an hour, or not for a day. Nurses saying hearing is last sense to go so I sing & joke.

Dr. Benvolio came by, looked in, sat down, and put a hand on my elbow while he looked at my mother.

"That plan we talked about," he said, and shook his head. "I think we'd better let her be."

"I agree."

"She really is so lovely," he said, and looked a while longer. "I'm glad we got to know her."

I think I can safely reveal now that last night we snuck a dram of "grape juice" to my mother. Nurses shocked, shocked!

Shifts changed. I went to a room downstairs the hospital had thoughtfully opened so that I could see my family. I came back up and pulled the non-recliner closer to my mother's bed.

"I'm gonna settle in here for a while," I told her. "Just saw the girls. They're fine. So excited—they met a guy in a cheesecake suit. They send their love. Elise is growing—how did you used to put it? 'Like a weed.' So athletic. And Paulina loves dressing up in pretty things, just like you. The sun was just starting to dip when I came up, this big bright ball painting the skyline orange."

I heard the cheeps and peeps of carts on the floor before Rosemary came in and smoothed a blanket over my mother's shoulders.

"Her temperature is down," she told me.

"What does that mean?"

"It won't be long now," she said. "If you want someone to be with you, call."

I phoned my wife. She wanted to rush over, but would first need to get someone to stay with our daughters. Then I called my mother's husband, who said he'd already said his own quiet good-bye. I see now that he didn't want to intrude on what he felt should be my mother's last moments with her son.

Heart rate dropping. Heart dropping.

I thought that I might climb once more onto the hospital bed to hold my mother, and have an arm around her shoulders when she took her last breath. I had looked into the sky and made a plea for that just a couple of nights before. But now I felt I should just sit before her and use every second to take in her soft face, her mild smile, and her smooth hands, which had begun to stop twitching. I was quite sure that my mother wanted me to stay back.

Dying is a solo act.

I don't much like euphemisms for death. But when her eyes stopped trembling I knew my mother had gone ahead.

I held my mother's hand until I could feel her fingers stiffen. I slipped out my hand carefully, made a sign of the cross, and kissed her fingers, and then I stood to kiss her forehead.

My wife arrived and saw that my mother was still and the room was silent. She put her arm around me and we began to cry. A look of peace had settled on my mother's face. She looked poised, serene, and regal. Her spirit had reigned in that room for days, and now it lingered.

We're sure my mother would have enjoyed the young doctor, curly-haired and clumsy as a puppy, who came in to certify that she was dead.

"You'll have to bear with me," he said. "This is my first time doing this."

"Ours too," we told him.

The young doctor took a long time to read through what looked like fine print in a text of instructions, the way most of us might read the booklet that comes with a new waffle iron. He took down my mother's gown and listened for a heartbeat or breath. He put a finger on her neck to feel for any pulse in her artery. Finally, he lifted my mother's eyelids and passed a light in front of her wide, brown, beautiful eyes.

This is that moment in which you see that someone you love is dead, just not sleeping. It is hard to see eyes that were once lively and expressive turn stony and cold. My wife and I looked, and then had to look away. We admitted to each other later that we'd each hoped and half expected my mother to flinch, blink, and say, "Did I nod off? What's going on?"

But the young doctor leaned back from her bedside and made notes. He mumbled something about all the paperwork he had to do, and that we—me, my wife, and my mother in her deathbed—had to be out of the room in just a couple of hours.

All of this sounds a little cold now, but it made my wife and me smile. I like to think some spark of my mother had touched us. She would have seen the young doctor, single-minded, slue-footed, and verbally klutzy, and been charmed. She would have told him, "Don't worry, dear. You're doing great. You're going to save a lot of people's lives someday."

I put my cheek against my mother's hand. I leaned over to kiss her forehead, which was already cool and smooth. I said nothing because I could think of nothing that I hadn't already said. My mother poured everything she was into me, and at the end, I tried to do the same for her. And she would have reminded me, we had daughters waiting a few blocks away.

I put my hand on my mother's cheek and told her, "I'll take it from here."

The heavens over Chicago have opened and Patricia Lyons Simon Newman has stepped onstage.

She will make the face of heaven shine so fine that all the world will be in love with night.

28

Worst: telling our daughters. Oldest was flinty, youngest sobbed. But guess which one cried long into the night . . .

The next day, we rode out to the cemetery in which my mother wanted to have her ashes interred, in a small vault next to her late husband Ralph.

A woman in a dark suit with a permanent crease of sympathy across her forehead told us, "And we'll have Patricia right next to Nicholas and below Angela."

"Who are they?"

Flustering and gulps followed.

The somber woman rolled her eyes over an old folder.

"Your mother is Patricia Costakis. . . ."

I thought of my Irish mother who had three Jewish husbands, but no time for Mr. Costakis.

"My mother had four last names in her lifetime," I told her. "That's not one of them."

232 • Scott Simon

We signed papers and checks, to return for the interment in two days.

The couple who ran the cremation service turned out to be delightful, dressed in black but warm and funny. They called themselves "post-health-care professionals," and reminded me of my mother's belief that you can meet the nicest people under the most unexpected circumstances.

Cemetery at first confuses my mother w/ another Patricia. Almost interred next to total stranger. Why not make new friends?

29

**So much important flotsam in the wake of a life.
USPS says fill out change-of-address for deceased.
Wish I knew to where . . .**

**Just found my mother's Chicago voter's
registration card. Looking forward to using it
for many years!**

We went through closets in my mother's apartment, to laugh and
weep over old photos, letters, souvenir ashtrays, and scraps of
life.

I got my hair cut for my mother's interment. If I ever begin a
sentence with, "My mother would have wanted me . . . ," the truth
is: all I know for sure my mother would have wanted is for me
to get my hair cut. I got my hair cut before every bar and bat
mitzvah, and confirmations, my graduations, anyone's funeral,
my wedding, and her weddings.

"If the air raid siren went off now," I used to tell her, "you'd turn to me and say, 'Just enough time for a haircut.'"

And now I got one for her interment. Ashes to ashes, dust to dust, snip by snip.

The man in the chair right across from me was having his head shaved, and when his barber lifted a steamy towel from his brow I could see that he was one of the most famous athletes ever to play in Chicago.

He had his head shaved and rubbed, then stayed for half an hour, talking baseball with everyone who approached. He was considerate and charming, and when I got out of the shop I reached for my phone to call my mother to say, "Guess who I saw getting a haircut right across from me?"

I caught myself before I could call, but only just. This will happen for the rest of my life.

I got so many thousands of messages in the days that followed from people who said they had read or heard about my mother during our last days together and had been entertained and inspired by her, that it was sometimes a little easier to pick out the few criticisms. Those baffled me a little. I hadn't shared intimate medical details. I hadn't implied—and this was important to her—that my mother's death was any kind of tragedy. She had lived a long, full, and rewarding life, and then she died. I posted messages in which I confided some of my fears, and shared some of my mother's sagacity and wit as we went through what is, after all, a universal experience.

My mother died and I mourned. That's as much a part of life as love and taxes. Why be quiet about it?

I don't confuse Facebook "friends" or Twitter "followers" with the old friends I still have from the fourth grade, or the close friends with whom I went through wars. But I think social media expands the exposure and experience we have that forms our ideas, beliefs, perspectives, and feelings. The Internet, television, radio, books—and for that matter, stone tablets, Homeric poems, Irish folk ballads, and papyrus scrolls—have done that at different times, too.

Life-changing experiences can transform and teach us, and move us to share what we believe we've learned. We want to shout the news of a birth into the heavens and place the face of someone we've loved and lost in the stars. We want people to *know.* It is an utterly human response, imperfect but invaluable.

It also seems to me that as her life wound down, my mother was inspired (I deliberated a long time over that word; I think it's right) to pass on memories, lessons, and insights with the sharpened perspective of someone who was already beginning to see into whatever is next. The wisdom that my mother had won over a full, fascinating, and involving life hardened and glowed into a few words that she wanted to share: share with me and my family for sure, but also, I can say with a son's certainty, pass on to others, too. She was an old showgirl who gave a great last performance and died with her son by her side. That's an event to be shared with the jubilation of a birth.

My mother had a grand memory for jokes, old movies, and family stories. But as I thought through her life by her side, I finally saw that what helped her keep going was a gift to be able to forget.

My mother forgot old slights, insults, and outrages. She tried to leave behind a lot of tragedies, hurts, and mistakes. My mother was the only child of parents who often couldn't be bothered with her. She loved and married a man who drank himself into a nosedive. She lost a daughter. Her mother took her life when she needed her most. She had to take her son and jump out of her marriage before her husband made them all crash. My mother's heart was shaken and broken a thousand times. She often felt lonely and abandoned. She looked over the edge. A lot of people would have used any one of those events to define and immobilize their lives, but my mother kept *moving*. She lived through a lot and she left a lot behind.

There are some weeks I cover the news in which I do not understand how anyone lives to the age of twelve. All of the wars, tragedies, car wrecks, stupid accidents, and stupendous diseases! We see people die in the sky from terrorist attacks, and slip in their bathtubs. As my wife puts it, "Life is always on a ledge."

So seeing a mother live into her eighties is a blessing a lot of children don't receive. But a mother's death is an irreplaceable loss. Spouses and friends may nag us in a friendly (or not so) way. No one else can tell us with the matchless mandate of a mother that we have worn the wrong shirt, done the wrong thing, worked too many hours, or been unfair to someone who deserves better.

A mother's death also makes us realize: we're next. It resets the clock we keep on our own lives. It reminds us not to let our best loves, dreams, vows, and promises dry up and die.

It is necessary to lose our mothers to finally grow up. There is no need to hurry this along; it happens too soon in any case. But there is some wisdom that we can't learn until our mothers have let go. There are lessons that only loss, grief, and responsibility can give us. Our mothers know this too, and the thought even gives them comfort. They will take a seat and watch us, as they once watched our first steps or school plays, until that day (which also comes too soon) that we let go of the hands of our children and join our mothers. They pour everything they are into us, then stand us on our own.

Day of my mother's interment. Left hand quavered so much, daughter had to help w/ buttons. Glimpse of my future.

30

Someone I've found difficult to like sent me such a nice note on my mother I forget why I didn't like him. Thanks Mother.

A few months after my mother died we were in Normandy, where my wife has family, and we spent a weekend in Paris. We inveigled our daughters into an art museum on the promise of ice cream.

I asked for directions to the Lautrecs. We found *La Toilette* on an upper floor of the Musée d'Orsay: the woman's slack, pale back and slender arms, her auburn bun of hair, the clutter of petticoats, the crumpled boots, the smudged tin tub.

"Grand-mère and I used to look at pictures of this painting," I told our daughters. "She said it was like looking through a keyhole," and as soon as I used the phrase I realized that children growing up now might have never seen a keyhole. "Do you think this woman is tired?"

Our daughters stopped for a moment. They had seen Degas's bronze horses and ballet dancers at the far end of the long room, and wanted to scamper off to look up some bronze butts.

"Maybe," they said. "I guess."

It rained as we left, and we waddled on the heels and toes of our rain boots along the walkway next to the Seine. The streets were quiet, shiny, and clear.

"Rain makes the city so quiet and personal," I told them.

We wandered into an old church. Candles gleamed and quavered in the gray light that flickered through the stained-glass windows. I remembered the times my mother and I had just walked and wandered into churches in neighborhoods we didn't know well in cities we loved, and lit candles for people we cherished.

"Dad," I'd suggest.

"Of course," my mother would say, and tilt the vigil light so I could reach it. "I put in a dollar, so we can do a few. Auntie Chris?"

"Sure!"

"She'd like that. We'll tell her. Who else?"

"Ernie Banks. On the Cubs," I'd remind her.

"Why not?"

So I sat on a pew in the Paris church and watched my wife and daughters walk from statue to statue, saint to saint. I smelled the white wax as it melted in short green glasses, and realized that all the reminders of my mother didn't make me sad. They gave me pleasure; they made me smile. She had made me laugh a lot, even when I angered, failed, or disappointed her. She held me close, and let me go. She taught me kindness, jokes, and grace. I'd had the chance, in our last days together, to tell her that I loved her, and I had the chance to show her. My religious convictions are chaotic and irreconcilable. But I hope I can recognize a blessing.

I got up and began to look for the statue of a saint I could identify and found one at the back of the church. The old stone saint was a handsome, silvery man who held a baby in his arms.

"You should take Joseph to be your patron saint," my mother had told me a few years before.

"Because he was a Jewish father who thought his kid walked on water?"

"A father who adopted and loved his child," my mother reminded me. "And believed whatever his wife said."

I knelt on a worn felt railing in front of the marble Joseph. I smiled to remember and said *thank you, thank you*—I suppose it was a prayer—and my daughters saw me and walked over, grinning with a surprise.

"Let's light a candle for Grand-mère," they said. *Let's.*

We don't become the people we are all at once. But if we are lucky, every love, laugh, and loss puts a wrinkle in our hearts to make us distinctive. All the wrinkles, reverses, and trials will teach us a little and give our lives purpose and meaning. By the end, my mother had put such clear purpose into her life that it can be remembered in just a few lines, written on a small piece of paper, and kept in a pocket for our children:

Write thank-you notes. Tip well. Sing. Drink responsibly. Remember that good manners cost nothing, and open doors. Reach out to someone who is lonely. Make them laugh. Help people smile.

Acknowledgments

Our whole family is grateful for the kindness and support of Cindy Barnard; Deann, Lanie, and Rick Bayless; Cyndi Brandenburg; Suzanne Brandenburg; Andy Carvin; Dr. Neil Cherian and the Cleveland Clinic; Fr. Charles Faso; Whitney Frick; Marcos Galvany and José Solis Betancourt; Matthew Gelbin; Wen Huang; Dave Isay; Wayne Kabak; Kathy Layne; Ken and Lucy Lehman; David Lyons; Sue Lyons; Kee Malesky; Daniel and Ronette McCarthy; Bob Miller; Steve North; Sarah Lucy Oliver; Peter Sagal; Marc and Maureen Schulman; Fanchon and Manny Silberstein; Leona Richard Simon; Margaret Low Smith; Kevin Sullivan; Megan Sullivan; and the West End Public Library.

We have suffered a few more losses in the months since my mother's death. We hold my aunt Izetta Magazine and my wife's father, Edouard Richard, close in our hearts. My mother saw no distinction between two- and four-legged family members. So we also use this space to treasure all the comfort and companionship our cat, Leona, has given our family.

Thousands of people have sent us messages over Twitter, Facebook, and other platforms. Thank you to all those who took the time to write (and still do). You have given us much comfort; I hope we have returned at least a little. I think my mother would be particularly delighted to know how students at the Bignay National High School in Valenzuela City, the Philippines, read her words, and wrote essays in response. The messages I have traded and enjoyed with students there show us how new platforms may help bring us into each other's lives.

Many have asked us where they might make a contribution to honor my mother. She would welcome the chance to help support the Anti-Cruelty Society, the Art Institute of Chicago, the Chicago Public Library Foundation, and the Goodman Theatre. And I am pretty sure she would tell people they can honor her memory most by reaching out today to someone who is lonely.

The care and consideration that ICU nurses and technicians, to whom this book is dedicated, gave to my mother was profound, intimate, and *routine*. They have cared for hundreds more people with equal, matchless kindness since then. They are heroes and inspire us.

And I dedicate my life to Caroline, Elise, and Paulina. They are my loves, and my life.

SSS